Chasing Shadows

The Search for Rod Evans

The Stairway Press Edition

Adrian Jarvis

Chasing Shadows: The Search for Rod Evans
The Stairway Press Edition

STAIRWAY PRESS—APACHE JUNCTION

Cover Design by Guy D. Corp, www.GrafixCorp.com

STAIRWAY≡PRESS

www.StairwayPress.com
1000 West Apache Trail—Suite 126
Apache Junction, AZ 85120 USA

FOREWORD

IN MY RECOLLECTION (which is questionable, but let's run with it), it was one of a stack of cheap 45s purchased during a blowout sale at Grant's Drug Store on Balboa Avenue, Clairemont, California in 1970. The slate-grey label felt foreboding and the label name intriguing—*Tetragrammaton* was difficult to parse for an 8-year old, but it seemed to hold secrets I was eager to pursue. I'd heard the song barreling from my mom's car radio and it struck me as particularly "cool," which is an important commodity for a young kid trying not to be a nerd. I remember gasping when I saw the record in the pile at Grant's at least a year after I'd first heard it, and I was astonished that it was available for a paltry sum; it was a prize to be treasured.

Perhaps the hook's melodic similarity to the bridge of *A Day In The Life* exerted some sway on my subconscious? (I was a Beatles freak above all.) The groove was relentless, the guitar sounded like the devil, the fact that organ featured so prominently in the arrangement was definitely appealing (that was my instrument from age 7)—and while the record exuded a sinister mystery to me (I think the wolf calls at the top are to blame), the lead vocal was entirely earthly and earthy, strong and swaggering with an enviable and easy confidence. It felt like something to aspire to. I loved this song and its vocal, flat out. I still do.

Hush was the very definition of a killer single but I somehow didn't delve further into Deep Purple's catalog at the time, and I remember being puzzled when a clearly different version of the band began to conquer FM radio. I dug those later radio hits like mad, but they had the strange function of freezing *Hush* in its time for me, relegated to a dusty drawer of rock history, and I never did explore those early albums. Alas, there is too much good music around and too many other obsessions to chase.

To discover years later that the singer who had been a part of such an above-ground phenomenon as Hush was also the singer in such a below-the-radar (and, to me, wildly intriguing) band as Captain Beyond was a good learning moment for me, an exercise in smashing preconceptions. I now sit watching a video of Rod Evans fronting Captain Beyond live and I ponder the vagaries of the rock business—this is a performer who could have and should have made a larger splash. But he certainly left a major imprint on the psyche of this former 8-year old, and I welcome the existence of the book you're reading, because his is a story that holds particular fascination for me. His story deserves to be told.

All our stories do, of course.

—Mike Keneally

American guitarist, keyboardist, vocalist and composer, Michael Joseph Keneally has toured the world with many artists and ensembles, including Frank Zappa, Frank's sons in Z, Steve Vai, Joe Satriani and is a touring guitarist for Brendon Small's Dethklok. He composed the 52-minute suite, *The Universe Will Provide*, which was performed and recorded with Holland's Metropole Orkest. Among many other bands and configurations, he fronts the acclaimed Mike Keneally Band.

Prelude: Happiness

BIRMINGHAM'S NEC ARENA was buzzing that night. Pre-gig, the vast foyer was packed with eager rock fans. Most of them were male and most of them were relatively advanced in age. Under the circumstances, that was not unexpected and, anyway, both myself and my friend Tony fitted those descriptions. I was dressed in my standard gig attire of jacket and relevant t-shirt. In this case, the latter bore a representation of the cover of the classic Rainbow album, Rising. A dark, gothic fantasy depicting a giant fist thrusting out from a raging sea to grab at the multi-coloured curve of that strange and beautiful atmospheric phenomenon from which the band took its name, it is an image that resonates throughout my late childhood and adolescence. As an encapsulation of its time (1976) and genre (heavy rock), it is nigh on perfect. Pompous, iconic, operatic, redolent of magic and the sagas of some Tolkienesque Middle Earth, it is a pretty accurate visual representation of the thundering guitar, pounding rhythm section and baroque keyboard stylings of the music to be found on the record it originally protected.

Tony and I were there to celebrate the career of Ritchie Blackmore, lead guitarist of Rainbow and before that, Deep Purple, two heavy rock Goliaths, the sounds of whom had done much to condition the way I see the world. Blackmore had spent most of the previous twenty years plying his trade in a largely acoustic outfit that traded in minstrel-like melodies and medieval poetry. The gig which Tony and I were attending was one of a handful that were to possibly be his final farewell, at the age of seventy one, to riff-based rock and roll. It was the last of the series and the only one held in the UK. Blackmore would be fronting a scratch band, although it would carry the Rainbow moniker. Being there as a member of the audience was something of a privilege.

It was two months and a few days since the New York trip. Blackmore had missed that one, so this was a chance to make up for his absence. All the other surviving members of the classic Deep Purple line-ups had been in New York—well, all but two, one because (not for the first time) he had not been invited and one because...but, hold on: I'm coming to that...this Rainbow gig would at least allow me to claim that I had seen most of the main players within the space of a few weeks.

It was also a coda of sorts. The quest was over. This was an epilogue, albeit that it appears here as a prologue. It was a chance to simply enjoy the music. Blackmore had made it known that he intended to play not only Rainbow but Deep Purple classics. My main narrative had already reached its ambiguous climax; I felt that I had the Holy Grail in my hands, although many others may have disagreed. This was the return to Camelot.

I had known my companion for the evening, Tony, for years. We had worked together in the Birmingham area, but I had headed off to East Anglia a decade or so earlier and we had only seen each other occasionally in all that time. The gig, then, was also the revival of a friendship. That, after all, is what the Holy Grail is all about: renewal, resurrection. Blackmore's temporary revival of his rock career came at a moment of revivification for me, too.

While waiting for the gig to start, we had a beer and chewed the fat. In the background, a band advertising some drink or other played on a small stage in the foyer, producing sounds that clearly tried to imitate those of Rainbow, without quite getting them right. Our conversation ranged over a hundred different topics—our jobs, our families, what whatsisname was up to these days—but it was not difficult to spot that what we were really talking about was endings and new beginnings. New opportunities. New homes. New ways of living. Don't let anyone tell you that middle age is all about being settled and boring: it may just be the most turbulent part of your life.

Beers quaffed, we took our seats. We were a good distance from the stage, but that did not matter. The experience we were about to have was not, after all, going to be primarily visual. The supporting band, Mostly Autumn, came on; they played a mixture of heavy rock and folk, with song titles that might have featured on Frodo Baggins' 'Trip to Mordor' iPod playlist (Tony dryly remarked that he, 'was beginning to spot a pattern' as yet another sword and sorcery epic was announced). Still, they were tight and entertaining and got us in the mood for the main event.

It was not long in coming. The house lights dimmed. A huge arc that spanned the stage, a neon rainbow, popped into vibrant life and the first few staccato bars of the opening number, a reworking of Deep Purple's 'Highway Star', filled the air. The vocalist, a relative unknown who was skilled at sounding like all the other vocalists with whom Blackmore had ever collaborated (the male ones, at least), was the chief link man between band and audience. Blackmore himself was an unassuming presence, a black-clad figure at stage left wielding a white Fender Stratocaster. He never tried to make the show about him, always allowing the music to be the star.

Over the next two hours, the thousands of his fans who were packed into the NEC Arena were treated to a set consisting of many of his finest moments. From his Rainbow back catalogue came standards such as 'Since You Been Gone', 'Man on the Silver Mountain' and, from the Rising album, 'Stargazer'. Deep Purple supplied the opener and several rarely performed songs such as 'Mistreated', 'Burn' and 'Child in Time'.

The evening came to a close, as was inevitable, with a run-through of 'Smoke on the Water'. Even people who have no interest in Deep Purple know it to be the band's most famous track. It had to be that one. What else could it be? It has been said that its main riff 'conquered America'. Maybe it did, but it has done a lot more than that; it is recognised all over the world. It is simple, mesmerising and—what is less frequently remarked upon—endlessly catchy. As those inimitable notes wended their way from guitarist's fingers to audience's ears, I was struck, among all the shouting and singing along from the, by now, frenzied crowd, that this might be the last time that the man who wrote that riff would play it in public—in the context of a rock gig, anyway. For someone like me, it was a poignant moment.

And what is that, exactly? 'Someone like me'? Well, you'll find that out, too.

Tony is someone like me and we were both abuzz as I drove him back home, chatting like excited teenagers. Favourite moments? Standout tracks? Surprises? Had age caught up with Blackmore a bit? We both agreed 'yes' but averred that he could still blow 99% of guitarists off the stage. We were two men whose long lost younger selves had re-emerged for a magic moment.

I dropped Tony off and headed up to Karen's place in Nottingham. I didn't get back to my own home until the next day, a Sunday. I stopped off at a local supermarket to pick up some supplies for the rest of the weekend. I was still wearing that t-shirt under my jacket.

'You can wear a Rainbow thing all you like.'

Absorbed by the fruit that I had been weighing up, I looked around for the voice and found myself confronted with an older guy whose sizable gut was being restrained by a t-shirt that celebrated a different, but no less heavy, band.

'You like them?' I asked.

'Love 'em!'

'I saw them in concert last night.'

'I didn't know they were still going.'

I explained that, technically, they weren't, but that Ritchie Blackmore had come out of rock retirement to…etc, etc….

'I first saw them back in '77,' the guy said to me.

'Really?'

'They were touring that one—"Rising". Excellent!'

He looked wistful, as though reliving a memory.

'Blackmore,' he finally pronounced, 'What a guitarist! A genius! Can he still play as well as he used to?'

The truthful answer to that question was 'probably not', but I was not interested in strict truth at that moment. I preferred to recount the myth of Ritchie Blackmore, the musical mega-talent, rather than dwell on the facts of Ritchie Blackmore, the old man who was not quite as fast as he used to be and had probably only played those few gigs to get himself an instant pension fund. I talked about rock perfection and described a few moments from the gig to prove my point.

'If I'd known about it, I would have got a ticket.'

'It was sold out.'

'I'm not surprised! Rainbow have still got a lot of fans out there.'

'Deep Purple are my favourite band,' I told him, 'Blackmore played a few of their tracks last night, too.'

'I always liked them. I was there for all of that stuff when it was first released. Great days!'

'I'm a bit younger than you, then. I had to catch up with a lot of it later on. It was already part of the rock canon before I first heard it.'

'I suppose being older has got to have some advantages.'

He was right, of course. Much of what he said commented on the quest upon which I had recently embarked, although neither the Rainbow gig nor the impromptu supermarket chat with him were strictly parts of it. Nevertheless, that weekend in cameo form encapsulated the way it had all happened. It had not been a quest in any conventional sense, although it had certainly involved quite a bit of travel. It had been punctuated by gigs and conversations with old rockers, most of whom were connected to me only by a shared passion for the music.

I left the guy to his reveries and moved on, happy to have met another kindred spirit and happy that the quest had helped me to understand what that meant. It had been a revelation long in the gaining—and who would have predicted that it would come in, of all places, New York?

But it had begun in altogether less auspicious surroundings some years earlier and the central figure had not, in fact, been Ritchie Blackmore, but a very different character who had also given up rock and roll, without showing any inclination to take it up again.

His name? Rod Evans.

1—Listen, Learn, Read On

THE IDEA TO search for Rod Evans was hatched in the sauna of a sports centre in the grounds of one of Britain's top public schools.

I was visiting my friend Loz. We had just been for a swim, our efforts practically defining the word 'perfunctory'. After a few lengths that did nothing to increase our fitness or decrease our BMIs, we were having what we kidded ourselves was some well-earned relaxation time. We were talking, as men in early middle age tend to do, about where we had come from and where we wanted to go. If the atmosphere in that small wooden room had not been broiling from hot coals, it would have been smoky from pipe dreams.

One thing we agreed on, though, was that we both wanted to take some kind of journey, to achieve something, to have some kind of memorable experience. I was aware even then that we could not have been more clichéd men-in-the-grip-of-a-mid-life-crisis if we had tried. Nevertheless, I proposed an 'adventure'. What it would be, I did not know. Neither was it necessary that I should, since it would never happen anyway. It was intended purely to give our imaginations a reason to keep telling our bodies that their ever-greater sacrifices were worthwhile.

At some point in the conversation, the notion of discovering something was mooted (in our minds we had transformed into a pair of corpulent Indiana Joneses) and then one of us, I forget who, suggested that we be the ones to finally track down Rod Evans.

I fully concede that we were not obvious candidates for this kind of escapade. Loz was Head of Art at the aforementioned public school. I was Head of English somewhere similar. We were both educated to post-graduate level, although neither of us had gained our qualifications by undertaking what the quest ended up being—something like a piece of investigative journalism.

We were both also mad fans of the band Deep Purple. We were more than fans, if I'm honest. We were Deep Purple geeks. Hardcore fans. The difference between a fan and a hardcore fan is open to debate, but, for me, it comes down to this: a fan likes the output of a band, author or whatever, and that's it. A hardcore fan, by contrast, will go to a whole different level, investing time in finding out about the object of devotion's life and amassing a collection that includes not just everything created by that person or persons, but rarities, variant texts and even context material.

Loz and I both fell into the latter category.

We both owned all of the band's music and had both attended many of their concerts—although, strangely, never, at that point, together. One of our main methods of keeping in touch was to play a text message game in which the first move was for one of us to send a snippet of Deep Purple lyrics to the other; the next move was for the other to send back the next line and then the third move was for the original one to send the next line and then...you get the picture. It was like a form of hard rock tennis.

So, when the heat of that sauna suggested the enticingly exotic prospect of an adventure, there was something oddly inevitable about one of us saying, half-jokingly:

'Hey! What about looking for Rod Evans?'

Rod Evans: a rather ordinary-sounding name for a hero. But hero he was. At least, to us, being the original lead singer with Deep Purple. He had not been heard from—so we thought—since 1980. No-one, as far as we knew, had a clue where he was or what he was doing. To the hardcore Deep Purple fan community he had become almost mythical, Mr. E the Mystery, a lost Holy Grail waiting to be rediscovered. On the face of it, embarking on that quest fitted Loz's and my requirements perfectly. As an experienced academic researcher, the idea appealed to me, but, more so, strangely, as a devotee of cryptic crosswords, I relished a puzzle. I wondered idly what a cryptic clue for 'Deep Purple' might be…'Penny and crazy peer led up rock formation (4,6)', perhaps? Or 'Group neither superficial nor simple (4,6)'? One way to characterise the journey we intended to take would be to see it as the solving of those clues….

But, I'm getting ahead of myself.

That sauna was not where the quest truly began. Not for me anyway. It began much earlier. Much, much earlier. The film needs to run in reverse for a while. You need to watch me open the sauna door and walk backwards to the pool before propelling myself feet-first up and down it for a few minutes. You need to watch me climb out of the pool and immediately dry out. You need to watch me drive home led by my car's tailgate as I do my party piece of only glancing at my direction of travel every so often in a mirror. You need to watch me change shape, my face thinning out, my body losing musculature, my hair growing back, my glasses passing through numerous fashions before resolving themselves into a pair of cheap-looking plastic NHS frames. You need to watch me strolling around the quads of Oxford with my face pointing the wrong way, studying literature by day and performing my favourite magic trick of filling beer glasses up from my mouth by night. You need to watch me diminish in size as the years fall away and I arrive back in my hometown of Stafford in England's West Midlands. Finally, you need to watch me walk backwards out of a certain shop and stand there staring at it, taking in its name for the first time, 'Lotus Records'.

You can start running the film in the right direction now.

Lotus Records.

It was the type of shop that simply would not exist these days. It was to be found down a side street. From the outside, it wasn't

9

much to look at: an unprepossessing facade with a naff brown and orange logo and windows that gave a view only of a gloomy interior. It would be nice to report that walking through the door (re-tracing the steps I had just taken in the opposite direction) was to enter an Aladdin's Cave, but, frankly, it wasn't. Inside, the place was dark and dusty. Racks displaying the empty covers of twelve inch vinyl LPs were the only furniture. Facing the entrance was the small hatchway of a counter, in front of which could be found, in neat alphabetical files, seven inch singles. These mostly featured an 'A' side you might pay for and a 'B' side nobody would. The walls were always festooned with posters and cardboard cut-outs advertising latest and forthcoming releases.

This was the early 1980s. I was a schoolboy of twelve or thirteen. Both of those statements need some expansion because the intersection of date and circumstance did much to condition the person I was then and, as a consequence, the person I am now.

We are used to looking back on the eighties as a golden age of hedonism when the yuppie was king and the only things bigger than mobile phones were the expense accounts that paid for them. But that really describes the late eighties. The early eighties were a whole different story. They were the years of industrial collapse, of rising unemployment, of riots in British cities and of an invasion of Afghanistan that was less a president's folly than a reason to fear a nuclear holocaust—if nuclear weapons had even been necessary given how much the early eighties already had an air of the apocalypse about them. I remember wondering why I was bothering with schoolwork since my chances of ever getting into paid employment were next-to-zero.

The early eighties was also the time of the New Wave of British Heavy Metal. I don't know when, or by whom, that phrase was coined; I only know that it could be taken as the title of the last occasion in music history that hard, heavy, often unlistenable, music was considered to be the Next Big Thing. Some of its exponents survived and went on to great things—Iron Maiden would be the pre-eminent example. Other bands fared less well. I remember a compilation of NWOBHM tracks called 'Metal for Muthas' hitting the market. Apart from the lengthy debates it provoked amongst myself and my friends about whether the strange word in its title should be pronounced 'mewthas' or 'mothers', it showcased a number of bands who were confidently expected to storm the charts—a feat they almost all signally failed to accomplish. Some, like Samson, had already achieved a respectable following, while others, such as Ethel the Frog and Toad the Wet Sprocket, were notable only for their manifest knowledge of Monty Python's more obscure sketches. Most were forgotten as quickly as any question of what a 'mewtha' might actually be.

My first encounter with heavy metal, or heavy rock, or whatever we end up calling it, came via a friend of mine named Paul. Much of my early eighties were passed in Paul's bedroom listening to his growing collection of NWOBHM albums and singles. In one of those vain attempts to fit in that characterise adolescence, I started professing a love for the music myself and bought as much of it as my meagre financial resources could stretch to. The first single I ever bought—I recall it distinctly—was 'Hellbound' by Tygers of Pan Tang, the first album was Iron Maiden's eponymous first effort—at that time their only release to date. But, despite my developing a mini-obsession with the 'Tygers' that saw me amass a small collection of their singles that would probably be quite valuable if it still existed, my heart wasn't really in it. I wasn't very inspired by any of it.

For a start, there was something very limited about the oeuvre of the average NWOBHM band. Every song seemed to either have 'hell' or 'run' in its title. The lyrics were fixated on evil; not every day, banal, evil, but evil of grand, video nasty proportions. The Diamond Head track, 'Am I Evil', summed it all up, being a tale of bloody revenge for violent, horrific murder. On top of this, I felt alienated by the culture surrounding these groups. Remember that I was just a suburban lad: all the long, unkempt hair, oily denim jackets and studded leather wristbands worn by heavy metal musicians seemed pretty threatening to me. All right, these days, we might more readily associate the look with gay chic, but, back then, it all had the whiff of danger and criminality about it.

Finally, though, the music, the lyrics, the approach, just didn't seem to chime with the times. Those posters and flyers that provided Lotus Records with its revolving and evolving wallpaper were often for non-heavy rock bands, bands that were engaged with social themes and political debates. It seems hard to believe now, in an age of bland, corporate pop that only has to appeal to particular 'demographics', but many musicians in the early eighties used the platform granted by their art to make very real, and often very angry, points about the rapidly decaying world around them. Stiff Little Fingers, Killing Joke, Crass, The Clash—they sang about stuff that mattered and their advertising—usually far from slick, but dynamic—made Lotus Records the place that it was. In the face of all that, the gothic fantasies of NWOBHM bands with names like Cloven Hoof and Demon Pact seemed…well, to be honest, a bit silly.

Still, I spent a lot of my time in Lotus Records, which, as far as I can remember, stocked nothing but heavy rock/metal and punk. I did this because—and this is something else about the place that now has the patina of another age about it—Lotus was one of those record shops you could just hang out in. You didn't have to buy anything. You could look at the album covers, chat to the staff about the music. You could learn. It was there that I began to find out more about Deep Purple.

As with heavy rock in general, I first came across Deep Purple at Paul's. He was not exclusively a fan of the NWOBHM; he also liked older rock, the rock from the bombastic seventies, rock that, even in those far off days, was spoken of with the reverence reserved for the legendary. It was at Paul's that I first came into contact with AC/DC, a band whose songs had a much-needed air of fun about them (even if they did sing about Hell—a lot) and it was there that I was first acquainted with the symphonic brilliance of Rainbow's magnum opus, Rising. But, above all, it was there that I first heard Deep Purple: the guitar riff to the all-conquering 'Smoke on the Water', the gentle organ intro to 'Child in Time', the nonsensical lyrics of 'Black Night'. These were all introduced to me via a compilation album called 24 Carat Purple of which Paul owned a copy.

Now, it needs to be said that, at the time, Deep Purple were no longer a going concern. They had split, apparently forever, in 1976 and, although they got back together again in 1984 (and, as I write, have, with one or two personnel changes, been together ever since), this prospect seemed distant indeed when I first encountered them at Paul's. They were gone, a bright flame that had burned for all too brief a time and then been snuffed out. Oh, yes, the various musicians who had made up the band were still around and still working—mostly, in different combinations, with each other—but Deep Purple itself was over. In a way, this was partly what intrigued me about them; they belonged to the pre-Armageddon generation when bleakness had yet to take over from brashness.

Their other appeal was the music. They never played the kind of thrashy drivel that was the stock-in trade of most NWOBHM practitioners. Their music, while it was as heavy as you could hope for, was elegant, full of complex arrangements, twiddly riffs and surprising solos. They played amped-up rock and roll for certain, but there seemed to be something classical about much of their writing—baroque and roll if you like. Their long, jammy live pieces were also full of a sort of improvised jazz that could, and often did, go anywhere.

Lead guitarist—the aforementioned—Ritchie Blackmore seemed able, at will, to get whatever sound he wanted from his instrument. As for keyboard player, Jon Lord—well, there was a distinguishing feature for a start: this a rock band with keyboards. And he brought so much depth and subtlety to the music. Roger Glover's bass was a dependable foundation for the more showy instruments and Ian Paice can plausibly claim to be the greatest rock drummer ever. Overlaying it all was the scream, the war cry for don't-give-a-fuck abandon that was the voice of singer Ian Gillan. I made an immediate connection with it. This was music I could love!

Moreover, it was not without a political edge. A song like 'No No No' (from the Fireball album) was perhaps a bit unfocussed in its targets being, basically, a protest song about—you know—whatever. But look at the lyrics from 'Child in Time'. Writer Ian Gillan has claimed that this song is about the ever-present threat of nuclear war that bedevilled the otherwise sunny sixties. Sure, you can see a bit of that—especially in the last two lines—and Gillan recycled much of this imagery in his solo band's later, less successful, anti-nuclear song 'Mutually Assured Destruction'. But there is something more poetically troubling about these lyrics: who are the 'child in time' and the 'blindman', for instance, and isn't the image of someone taking random pot shots at the world less redolent of mushroom clouds than of Charles Whitman's shooting spree at the University of Texas a couple of years before the song was written? The song promises violent punishment for 'being bad'. Is it, then, a call for greater morality? Or, perhaps, greater political commitment? That it is still relevant can be seen by how closely it mirrors the horrific events of Columbine, another motiveless gun massacre and one in which the killers taunted their victims with theological questions—before pulling the trigger. Whatever we make of 'Child in Time', it is not a simple statement, but a challenge, both to the world in general and to its audience in particular.

Fuelled by my growing fascination with such songs, my priority number one became to own as much of Deep Purple's music as possible. So I hoarded away my pennies and kept an eye on Lotus Records' second-hand rack. One day, my luck was in; there it was, an as-good-as-new copy of Deep Purple's album Burn for only two pounds. I'll admit it—it wasn't just the music; I was also drawn to the cover. These days, Deep Purple album covers of the seventies might be held up as the acme of bad taste, but, as a callow teenager, I found them witty and (I'm loath to confess this now) stylish.

In most instances, they featured the band members in various unlikely settings. In Rock turned them into a faux Mount Rushmore, Fireball had them in profile within a flaming comet, Who Do We Think We Are put them in bubbles. Burn featured candles based on their heads, all lit while an eerie purple fog crept around and between them.

Added to such illustrations were album logos that always appealed to my sense of eye-catching design. From an early stage, the band's approach had been to place their name at the top of the front cover in lettering that was so small as to be almost invisible, but to foreground the name of the album. It was as though they were removing their own egos from the equation and letting the music speak for itself. Again, Burn was a winner, the title being rendered in curly, flame-inspired letters that I spent many subsequent hours attempting to re-produce.

I handed over my two pounds and took the album home. My parents' stereo (old enough to merit the archaism, 'gramophone') was not the greatest sound system in the world, but it was better than nothing and I carefully placed my booty on the turntable, positioned the needle, sat back and listened. The music was heavy, complex, involving but—er—bluesy and there was even a hint of something calypso-like on one track. It was wonderful, sure, but not quite what I had expected. Most seriously of all—what was wrong with Ian Gillan? There were two singers, apparently, one screechy, one souly, but neither sounding remotely like the guy I'd heard on 24 Carat Purple. It was only then that I checked the names of the band's membership. There was no Ian Gillan and no Roger Glover, but there was someone called Glenn Hughes (never heard of him!) and David Coverdale (of whom I had heard, but only as the lead singer of the then-currently-popular Whitesnake).

This was an epiphany. It was the realisation that there had not merely been one Deep Purple, but many different incarnations of the band—or different 'marks' as they preferred to call them—each with their own distinctive sound. It was like the moment I realised that there had been more than one Doctor Who. I discovered that Burn was by Mark III and that Gillan and Glover had belonged to Mark II. This begged a question: what had Mark I been like? My investigations began....

The problem was that I was stuck in the early eighties. You could not just get onto Wikipedia and find out everything you could possibly want to know about any subject you could possibly want to know about; the Internet still lay in a distant and unanticipated future. My only sources were whatever published material was available and, for a band that had split up in 1976, that was precious little. I had seen the covers of Mark I's albums as part of a montage on the back of 24 Carat Purple, but I had assumed they had been made by Mark II. The rock fanzine Kerrang was launched at around this time and included many references to the band, but they were almost all to Mark II, with an occasional detour via Mark III. It was as though Mark I had been airbrushed out of history.

My first break came in—where else?—Lotus Records. I discovered therein a copy of the album simply entitled Deep Purple. This had a gatefold sleeve, the outside of which was a monochrome reproduction of 'The Garden of Earthly Delights' by Hieronymus Bosch (pretentiously, the cover art was credited to that old master as though it were a bespoke commission) onto which a small photograph of the band had been inexpertly cut (literally) and pasted (literally). The interior was a flat purple colour and included notes on each of the songs—sort of a late 1960s equivalent of a DVD commentary. These were the kind of self-important musings that the band members probably later came to regret, but, to me, they were gold, including, as they did, references to two mysterious new characters, 'Rod' and 'Nicky'. It was my first indication of what Mark I had been.

My second came soon after. The people behind Kerrang decided to release a special issue devoted to Deep Purple, referring to them as 'Britain's Greatest Heavy Metal Band'. It was a good read, including a history of the band, reviews of all of their albums, interviews and some unsubstantiated speculation about whether they would ever get back together (a prospect which, at the time, seemed about as likely as walking to America—or mobile phones ever becoming a reality). Many gaps were filled in by that magazine, not least that Mark I had lasted from 1968 to 1969 and had consisted of the core trio of Blackmore, Lord and Paice, joined by Rod Evans and Bassist Nick Simper. I learned that this version of the band had released the studio albums, Shades of Deep Purple, The Book of Taliesyn and the aforementioned Deep Purple (often called 'The Third Album').

By now, the NWOBHM fad had fizzled out leaving nothing behind but the ashes of under-achievement and a slew of embarrassing lyrics. Duran Duran, Culture Club and numerous synthesiser duos were dominating the charts. Liking rock music defaulted back to the status of uncool. But I didn't care. In fact, I was inversely snobby about it, arguing that my tastes were my tastes and had not been handed down to me by the marketing department of some multi-national media conglomerate.

And so I could have gone on, joining the ranks of all the many thousands who kept that Purple flame burning through the years when the band itself was gone, treating its music like a collection of sacred relics, untouchable, increasingly legendary and never to be augmented.

I could have done that—but I didn't. Don't get me wrong: I never stopped secretly liking Deep Purple, but, suddenly, around 1983, I decided that I really should become an intellectual and intellectuals simply did not listen to heavy rock. So—it pains me to own up to this—I got rid of my heavy rock collection. I sold it. All those seven inch singles. All those twelve inch long-players. No more 45 and 33RPM. Iron Maiden would no longer torture my parents, the Tygers of Pan Tang became extinct, Rainbow stopped shining brightly...I even—God forgive me!—divested myself of that copy of the Third Album. I kept some things: namely, all of my other Deep Purple albums. I just could not bear to be parted from them. Why I chose to include my sole example of Mark I product in the cull I cannot say. Perhaps it just did not speak to me in the same way that the other stuff did. Whatever, it was symptomatic of the somewhat bitter-sweet relationship I have enjoyed with Deep Purple's first incarnation throughout my life.

I was just getting into my new intellectual phase of pretending to enjoy opera when the game changed decisively and forever. It was 1984. Others might have feared Orwellian nightmares, but I had begun the year by having my first ever snog and so I faced the coming twelve months with a fair, and wholly unjustified, degree of optimism. Still, something more unlikely, more seemingly impossible than even my first contact with the Alien Female Other was about to occur: Deep Purple reformed! Naturally, the line-up concerned was Mark II; Mark I and, in particular, Rod Evans, were well off the scene, for reasons that will become clear later. The effect on my life was seismic.

For a start, the band released an album. This not only introduced new Deep Purple songs into the world, but helped to reclaim the old ones: they were no longer fixed, unchanging stars in the cultural firmament, but organic entities that had fresh potential to grow, develop and seek out new audiences. This they could do partly through the shuffling process that naturally occurs when a catalogue is still growing and partly through live appearances, of which many were planned. To say that I was excited by all of this is an understatement of overstated proportions. My classical pretensions were quietly forgotten and I became, once again, a hardcore Deep Purple fan. Naturally, I tried to see them every time they came close to wherever I was living; this was invariably Birmingham.

My first gig was at the NEC Arena in 1993. It was a

momentous night not only for me, but for the band. Ian Gillan has gone on record as saying that it was the worst Deep Purple gig ever. He went so far as to block a CD release of it some fifteen years after the event, conveniently forgetting that a video and CD of the night, entitled Come Hell or High Water, had been available for a good while. The video included interviews with the band members (Ritchie Blackmore excluded, but Gillan very much included) commenting on the disastrous events of that evening. Roger Glover said that he was 'furious at what happened'.

And what happened was—well, to this member of the audience, not a lot, to be frank. From my vantage point somewhere in a row of seats to stage right I could only see some of what 'Come Hell...' would later reveal in more detail, but it was clear that, as the band came on at the start, Blackmore was absent. The other four duly got on with the intro to their opening number, 'Highway Star', but it remained, for some time, sans guitar. A few bewildered looks were exchanged on stage as the build up went on and on.

Eventually, someone made the decision to get going and a keyboards-only version of the song got underway. Blackmore finally emerged from backstage in time for his solo. At first, I wasn't sure that it hadn't all been a deliberate coup de theatre. But something wasn't right with the so-called 'Man in Black'. He wandered over to the edge of the stage and threw something—it was all a little indistinct from a distance. On the video, he is seen to hurl a plastic glass of water over one of the cameramen filming the show. Why he did so no-one seemed able to say. From there, however, the gig progressed well—certainly as far as I could tell.

What I couldn't know at the time was that—good, bad or indifferent—it was pretty much Blackmore's swan song with the band. Soon afterward, he left for good. Temporary stand-in Joe Satriani covered dates that were already booked, before a more permanent replacement was found in the shape of Steve Morse. The 'mark' of which he is a member is the one that I have seen most often in concert. Every time they have brought their show to the UK I have faithfully joined the crowds of the devoted to be blown away by their amazing virtuosity. I particularly enjoyed the show at Aston Villa Leisure Centre in 1996 to which I took a crowd of my friends and colleagues. The set list was dominated by numbers from the line-up's 'debut' album, Purpendicular; this was only one element that gave the show a freshness and vivacity that had begun to seep out of the Blackmore-dominated gigs.

Then there was the revival of Jon Lord's rock/classical crossover piece 'Concerto for Group and Orchestra' at the Royal Albert Hall in 1999. This was to commemorate the thirtieth anniversary of its original performance, a recording of which had been Mark II's first album release. It was a stunning evening of music—one that Blackmore, had he still been around, might well have nixed at planning stage. The orchestra-backed tour of 2011 gave me another memorable night at the NEC.

It was at that gig, perhaps more than any previous one I had attended, that I began to get a distinct sense of the composition of the audience. I had come directly from Karen's place in Nottingham and still wore the black suit-style jacket that I had taken to hers for the purpose of going out for dinner.

My two concessions to scruffiness were the t-shirt I had beneath it (not, I have to say, a Deep Purple t-shirt) and the trainers I wore at the bottom of my black trousers. My look may have been eccentric, but it could hardly have been described as 'rock 'n' roll'. Still, that didn't matter. I looked somewhat cooler than most of my fellow fans: and that is a comment on them, rather than me. For the most part, they were an aged bunch. What hair remained on the average head had long since lost its colour.

Rarely have I seen so many people at an event (that is not an antique fair) walking with the aid of sticks. There were younger people there, including a good number of teenagers, but they were mostly accompanying parents and their devotion to the band seemed like the supporting of a football team, passed on from one generation of a family to another with little in the way of reflection.

With some time to go before the support band (Cheap Trick) were due to take the stage, I, like most of the audience, loitered around the foyer. I queued for something to eat and drink—yes, the queue was orderly and well-behaved—and got myself a pie and mash with a cup of coffee.

Alcohol was available, but, since it is next-to-impossible to reach the NEC by any means other than car, not much was being consumed by the sensible crowd.

During the gig itself, I sat on a raked area to the left of the stage as I was looking at it. I was a little disgruntled at being so close to the action—for reasons of hearing preservation. The seats were not over-comfortable and I was flanked by a fat guy in (God knows why!) an Iron Maiden t-shirt and a bald old guy wearing a polar neck sweater.

Most of the audience sat at ground level in chairs arranged in neat rows, a fact commented upon by Ian Gillan during the gig. Anything like a 'mosh pit' was absent because it was irrelevant: no-one danced. A decent percentage of the aged audience couldn't have danced if they'd wanted to.

It is fitting that the one thing that most came home to me that night was how the gig was a barometer of my personal history. Nights like that, Deep Purple gigs, were punctuation marks in the passages of time that had raced through my early adulthood and maturity before heading ineluctably into middle age.

Those nights were dotted around the years through which the plot of my life twisted and turned in many directions, some predictable, others less so. Twisted and turned through marriage, divorce, job changes, house moves, travel, study. But, as the plot of my life thickened, sickened and slackened, the band was always the subtext.

They were my enthusiasm, my comfort, my hard-wiring back to the person I had once been. But there was always one loose end, one frustrating area of uncertainty, one dark place on the map. It had a name, a name that rose in my imagination to haunt me, like a nagging whispering voice at the back of my mind: Rod Evans.

Rod Evans.

And the question remained, the big, unanswered, question: what had become of him?

What on earth had happened to Rod Evans?

2—Bird Has Flown

ANYWHERE CALLING ITSELF 'The Record Shop' has to be taken seriously. After all, it could hardly be accused of misleading advertising. Just such a place exists and it was to there that I paid a visit in search of some context for the burgeoning Rod Evans quest. The shop is to be found down a side street in a quiet Norfolk town, just along from a big church. Surrounded by hairdressers and the like, it's a strange anomaly, somewhere that logic tells you should not exist, but it does, standing proudly and defiantly, embodying the principle that love and enthusiasm can trump profit as a reason for doing something.

Karen was my companion on this visit; Loz had taken our original conversation for what, in all honesty, it probably was, idle banter, and dropped into the background. Walking through the door of the place, I immediately found, is like travelling back in time. It is arranged so that the first thing the customer comes up against is the racks of CDs. It is weird to think that even this once cutting edge format looks increasingly archaic in the age of instant downloads. But it is positively space age compared with what I was really there to look at—the ranks and ranks of vinyl albums and singles that fill most of the shop. They are arranged alphabetically by genre, colour-coded labels inscribed with felt tipped pens demarcating one artist's work from another's.

It is important to point out that The Record Shop only bears a superficial resemblance to that other music emporium that has figured in our narrative, Lotus Records. That was a going concern selling the latest releases of the day, which had been produced using the most up-to-date technology available.

The Record Shop is essentially an antique stall. The guy who runs it—as, in his own words, 'a one man band'—is one of those engaging characters who serve the indispensable social function of valuing what once was and, in doing so, reminding us of where we come from and who we are. He's an aging rocker with an encyclopaedic knowledge of his favourite music and enough love for it to go chasing after rare recordings or attending concerts by obscure bands wherever they might be held.

While we were there, he told us about buying trips he had made to Holland during which he had picked up some posters caricaturing The Rolling Stones, which he was 'knocking out for a tenner a piece'. He was the ideal guide as I rummaged through the stacks of twelve inch LPs looking for inspiration.

I was there because the mystery of Deep Purple Mark I is given added dimension by the paucity of recorded matter on which that iteration of the band features. There are the three studio albums, of course, and the singles, some of which are stand-alone numbers that did not originally appear on any album. Then there is a clutch of BBC sessions that have emerged either as bonus tracks to 'remastered' re-releases of the albums or, more recently, on a dedicated compilation. But that is more-or-less it.

The only extant live material comes from a supporting slot recorded in California in 1968. Dominated by cover versions, it has little to say about the band's musical development, but does give the distinct—perhaps not entirely fair—impression that Evans was out of his depth as the frontman.

Apart from that, there is a small number of surviving TV clips. One, filmed in black and white on an oil-stained rooftop, has the band looking moody as they lip-synch to their version of the Beatles' 'Help'. Another shows them recording the instrumental 'Wring That Neck'; significantly, Evans is seen lying on the floor throughout, contributing nothing.

By far the most bizarre Mark I TV slot, however, is an early appearance on a programme based around the magazine Playboy. Bemusingly bad even by the standards of the time, it is chiefly of interest now for its comedy value.

Hugh Hefner is our host and he gets things off to a noisy start by saying that 'The Deep Purple are here' and ready to play something. 'The' Deep Purple then give us a brief account of the instrumental track 'And The Address' during which Rod Evans moves awkwardly about the stage like the less talented twin of Bez from the Happy Mondays. But he is practically Nijinsky compared to the crowd of young people jigging aimlessly about the studio and threatening at various points to crash into the stage. Hefner then talks to the band, receiving a guitar lesson from Ritchie Blackmore.

For some reason, Hefner treats the instrument like a new fangled piece of technology that old farts like him will never fully understand before having a short chat with Jon Lord; the keyboard player's urbane and witty remarks are a stark contrast to the general buffoonery going on around him. It must have come as something of a relief to the band to be allowed to get on with a live rendition of their latest hit, 'Hush'. Here Evans comes into his own, looking less ill-at-ease than his colleagues and giving a fine live performance. Watching the clips, though, it is obvious that Hefner and, presumably, his producers, felt themselves to be dealing with a gang of one-hit-wonders who would be off the scene as quickly as they had fluked their way onto it.

The Record Shop's Deep Purple collection is wide and, I was told, 'well rifled through'. I started on the singles. I was amazed to find copies of most of Mark I's output, including a couple of examples of their biggest hit, the aforementioned 'Hush' (B side: 'One More Rainy Day').

There was also a copy of the slightly later wah-wah infused flop 'Emmaretta' (sample lyric: 'Emmaretta, did you get my letter?') and even one of those paper bags with a hole in the centre containing Mark I's cover of 'River Deep, Mountain High'—which had not been released in the UK. I gave Karen a running commentary on these as I went through them. She pretended interest and, to her credit, pretended well; her taste is not really for rock music.

When I turned to the album racks, they yielded everything I had hoped for: copies of all three Mark I releases. I handled them as an archaeologist might handle a priceless treasure that he has just dug up from the soil of some ancient city. They were, after all, valuable—and on so many different levels. Materially, they had a price, of course, as biro-scribbled labels proclaimed.

They had a further value as relics from my own past. For a moment, the hands holding those large flat cardboard covers were thirteen years old again and the eyes scanning their designs did so from a perspective of child-like wonder. Finally, those pieces of vinyl were valuable because of what they were—artefacts. They were LPs and that, somehow, made them superior to any other musical platform. Nothing else is just so—well—satisfying as an LP. It has a sense of occasion about it which neither a CD nor a download from the Internet can hope to match.

Their cover designs are meant to be twelve inches square and immediate in their impact. They seem meanly diminished when encased inside the plastic box of a CD and are rendered completely irrelevant by iTunes and its ilk.

Don't misunderstand me: I love the convenience and easy access of both CDs and downloads. I am keenly aware, however, that those two more modern formats are a different experience from that given by vinyl. Pressing a button on a remote control has none of the interactivity of carefully placing a needle on a groove, especially when performing the brain surgery required to locate a particular track. A spinning record catches the light on its grooved surface, highlighting the quirks and irregularities of the disc. An LP is organic and unique.

A CD is an anonymous, corporate piece of plastic. A

download is a radio wave. The development of listening formats could be taken as a parable of how much can be lost when significant gains are made.

'You looking for anything in particular?' the owner asked me as I shuffled the albums like a giant pack of tarot cards—but ones that told the past rather than the future.

'It's the Mark I material that I'm most interested in,' I said.

I was holding The Book of Taliesyn at that moment, so I added: 'See that? Best Deep Purple cover ever.'

The owner looked at it with an expression that combined affection with wistfulness.

'It's a great album, too,' he said, 'But I like the early albums—they're as good as some of the later stuff; easily.'

'Do you know what happened to Rod Evans?' Karen asked.

That is typical of her—cut to the chase and get results. I've seen her talk the representatives of large corporations into giving her unprecedented deals and be grateful to her for it. It's hard to work out quite how she does it. She is living proof that there is such a thing as a Jedi mind trick.

'Well, he was on those albums,' the owner said, 'Afterwards…he did one or two bits and pieces. Not much.'

'Captain Beyond?' I offered, naming Evans' most prominent post-Purple project (we will hear much more about Captain Beyond later).

'Well, yes.'

The owner sounded a little uncertain. Perhaps we had strayed outside his area of expertise.

'Have you got any of that stuff?' Karen asked.

The owner busied himself searching in the album racks, coming back moments later with empty hands and a 'sorry'.

As setbacks go, this was minor. You can see and hear all the Captain Beyond you could ever want on Spotify and YouTube. I didn't need to own any of it.

'Nice that you're interested in that stuff, though,' the owner went on, 'Because a lot of those old rockers are still kicking around.'

'I know. Nick Simper's still doing some stuff,' I said—we'll hear much more about him later, too—before adding, 'and, obviously, Ritchie Blackmore's still doing his thing.'

'Yes, I went to see Blackmore's Night,' he said.

'Who's that?' Karen asked, slipping into the role of Doctor Who Assistant for a moment.

I explained that it was the renaissance-themed acoustic-rock and vaguely-folk band that Blackmore had formed after finally leaving Deep Purple in the early nineties.

'I didn't realise that they'd toured the UK,' I said, silently cursing myself for not getting to a gig.

'Oh, yes,' the owner replied, 'They were very good.'

'Where did you see them?'

'Cambridge. The place was only about two thirds full, but the audience enjoyed themselves.'

'They do some Deep Purple covers, don't they?' I said.

'Yes,' he said, 'and they do them well. But, you know, you hear stories about Blackmore refusing to do encores and things. He did three encores that night and stuck around to chat to the fans afterwards. Not at all what you'd expect. Candice Night [She is the band's singer and, not coincidentally, Mrs. Blackmore. I was later to hear her live as a backing vocalist at that farewell Rainbow gig] took the piss out of him something rotten. He went along with it. If it'd been Gillan, he would have had a guitar wrapped around his neck.'

I was reminded of that night in 1993 when the dynamics within Deep Purple had clearly become terminally complicated. That had not been a Blackmore who would have stuck around to chat to fans; he only begrudgingly stuck around to do the concert that several thousand of us had paid to see. Perhaps age had mellowed him. Or perhaps performing with his wife—who also happens to be gorgeous—is just a more satisfying experience than sharing the stage with a bunch of hairy guys.

I didn't buy any of those lovely vinyl albums. I suppose it's hypocritical of me to say so, but I had no means of playing them and, anyway, I already have all of the actual music they contain— it's on my computer having been downloaded from iTunes. But I felt that I should give the owner something for his interest and friendliness and so I bought a cheap 'unauthorised' documentary about Deep Purple on DVD. This had the virtue of containing a new interview with Nick Simper that I felt might be useful to my research.

Okay, so visiting The Record Shop had not actually got me any closer to finding Rod Evans, but it had helped me to get a greater understanding of what that phrase might mean. Was I really searching for Rod Evans as a living, breathing human being or was he more a symbolic presence? Was my search even going to be for Rod Evans or, in some way, for myself?

That question was yet to be resolved, but, as for Rod Evans, I decided that, in the absence of the man himself, I could, at least, try to get a sense of him though some sort of environmental resonance by re-tracing a few of the steps he took. I know that sounds exceptionally lame, but it was all I had to go on and it seemed like a sound way to proceed. What made it seem even lamer was that my most obvious first port of call was where Evans had been brought up, the not terribly picturesque English town of Slough.

In culture, popular and otherwise, Slough has made two notable marks. Memorably, it is the subject of a poem by John Betjemen, who called upon 'friendly bombs' to come and raze it to the ground. It is also the setting for the Ricky Gervais comedy, 'The Office', in which it is portrayed as a joyless, mean little place full of hopeless, unimaginative, directionless people.

My only prior acquaintance with it had been when I attended a training meeting at Eton College (which tends not to advertise the fact that it is located in such a dismal setting). On that occasion, I had driven past the 'Slough Trading Estate' road sign that is used at the start of 'The Office' as a subtle symbol of a wasted life. That day, moreover, happened to be one on which I had lost my voice due to laryngitis—which is not an advantage when the headmaster of a world famous educational institution walks up to you over coffee for a chat.

That trip had not been Rod Evans related, but the one on which I was about to embark was. Karen and I visited. We saw nothing of interest. We came home.

Still, for our purposes, the true origin of Rod Evans was when he joined Deep Purple. Enough has already been written about the formation of the band and, since this is not an objective biography of Deep Purple but a disguised paean to fanhood, a brief summary will do.

The founding father was Chris Curtis, ex-drummer with The Searchers who proposed to start a band called Roundabout. This would consist of himself, one Jon Lord on keyboards and a guitarist—an up-and-comer named Ritchie Blackmore had caught his eye—who, together, would form a 'core' around whom guest musicians could play as and when their contributions would be useful, the metaphor being of them jumping on and off the 'roundabout'.

Allegedly, Curtis, under the influence of a prodigious drug intake, became increasingly eccentric and left the project before a note was recorded. Lord and Blackmore, though, saw some potential in working with each other and decided to carry on, recruiting the bassist Nick Simper from one of Lord's old bands and, from a band called The Maze, a singer, Rod Evans, who thoughtfully brought with him a drummer, Ian Paice.

With a line-up in place, the name Roundabout was dropped—presumably because it no longer described the band's modus operandi—although the fact that the basic trio of Blackmore, Lord and Paice remained constant throughout the first three line-ups with singers and bassists being kicked out as job lots at odd intervals means that, arguably, the Roundabout idea never entirely went away.

Intriguingly, there is some confusion surrounding the whole matter of whether the name was ever actually used. On his MySpace page, Nick Simper suggests that 'Roundabout' was an invention of the band's management and was never seriously considered by the musicians themselves. This seems at odds with Jon Lord's recollections in a television programme from the mid-1990s called 'Rock Family Trees' in which he recalled a conversation with Chris Curtis about the name and, more importantly, its conceptual possibilities. An early—extremely rare—acetate single called 'Shadows' was also, apparently, released by the band as Roundabout.

Whatever the truth, Jon Lord has spoken entertainingly about the alternatives that were kicked around as a better possibility was sought. 'Orpheus' was one, thankfully vetoed, as was 'Concrete God', which sounds faux-political and, given the existence of Iron Butterfly and Led Zeppelin, rather conventional. In the end, Blackmore imposed 'Deep Purple' which happened to be the title of his grandmother's favourite song. Indeed, a search for 'Deep Purple' on iTunes these days will yield as many results for the song as for the band.

For reasons that only the band members could reveal, they opted to model themselves on the American group Vanilla Fudge. This begs a question. To whit: why would such a talented bunch of musicians feel the need to model themselves on anyone? If the Vanilla Fudge collection on Spotify is anything to go by, however, they did a good job because it is often difficult to tell where Vanilla Fudge ends and early Deep Purple begins.

But, it must be admitted—even by a hardcore fan—that there was always a streak of unoriginality in Purple. They have often gleefully admitted that some of their most popular songs, such as 'Black Night' and 'Child in Time', borrowed riffs from other people's tracks, while 'The Mule' (from the Fireball album) bears more than a passing resemblance to The Rolling Stones' hit 'We

Love You'. In the end, they even started to copy themselves, as certain formulas crept in to the writing of songs and the composition of albums.

But all of that was for the future; for now, fully rehearsed and suitably monickered, Mark I was ready to go. Job One seems to have been to get some product out into the market and, as was de rigeur for bands in the sixties, they recorded an album in almost no time at all.

What can be said of that album, Shades of Deep Purple?

The cover promises little with its curly sixties lettering and its photograph of the band sporting curlier collars and even curlier perms. It says much about this design disaster that it has been toned down on re-releases of the album and, on one occasion, dumped altogether in favour of a no less unsatisfactory painting of a Fender Stratocaster rising up out of the sea.

The photograph is, however, interesting in what it seems to reveal about the dynamics of the band. Ritchie Blackmore, absurd hairdo present and correct, looks almost apologetically mousy on one side of the image. Ian Paice is relegated to the bottom of the frame where he has every appearance of someone who has sneaked into shot unbidden and is only there because the picture editor has forgotten to crop him out. Jon Lord dominates the image, standing at its centre, an indication, perhaps, of his power within the band at this stage in its history. Only Rod Evans comes away with his dignity intact, sitting self-confidently in the bottom left hand corner.

Getting inside the cover and listening to the album now is not only to benefit from a knowledge of how the band would subsequently develop, but to realise just how primitive recording technology used to be. Even with these caveats in place, though, 'Shades' is a strange confection and, as an opening statement from a new band, a distinctly underwhelming one. Its flat and uninspired production dates it badly as does its tiresome use of sound effects to fill the gaps between songs. The Vanilla Fudge influence is very noticeable in all the psychedelic twirls and whirls and, because of this, anything like a distinctive Deep Purple voice can only be detected in places.

Half of the album actually consists of cover versions—which are performed with varying degrees of success. 'Help' is quite highly regarded by some commentators, and, if the hype is to be believed, was praised by the song's composers, Paul McCartney and John Lennon. To these ears, the slowing of the tempo leads to nothing being achieved other than the transformation of a light, poppy number into something ponderous and pretentious.

The run through of Cream's 'I'm So Glad' is entertaining enough, but suffers by comparison to the instrumental lead-in, 'Prelude: Happiness', that precedes it. As for 'Hey Joe'—really? Covering that well-weathered warhorse seems to have been tantamount to a rite of passage for sixties bands, but it must have been obvious even then that Jimi Hendrix had had the last word on the thing.

Of the 'Shades' cover versions it is 'Hush', the one undisputed classic from this line-up, that best stands the test of time. A chugging, moody four minutes of rock 'n' roll bombast, its evergreen quality perhaps comes from the fact that several later bands have more-or-less based their entire act upon it (The Charlatans being the most obvious example).

Released as a single, Hush was a huge hit in America—the band's biggest ever—and, even in 2016, still featured in the band's live set, despite Ian Paice being the only survivor from the line-up that recorded it. It is an indication of the success of 'Hush' that it is universally regarded as a Deep Purple song, the fact of it originally being someone else's work having slipped from the public consciousness.

If the album's cover versions are a mixed bag that have largely failed to retain much interest, the band's own compositions have not fared much better. 'And The Address' gets off to a promising start with some rumbles and strange keyboard sounds before all the instruments come in for one of those massive crescendos that would later become a signature feature of the band's sound. From then on, the tune is a slightly rockier version of something that would not be out of place on an LP by Herb Alpert.

Things get worse with 'One More Rainy Day' which belies its title with a fairly upbeat organ-led intro that, nevertheless, cannot prevent the chorus melody from being forgettably dirge-like; when it goes into a 'pah pah pah p-pah pah pah' refrain, the modern listener is very likely to lose all patience. 'Love Help Me' is frisky and fast-moving but insubstantial.

One original song, however, does stand out, pointing the way to the future while sounding like nothing else on the album. That song is 'Mandrake Root'. In one respect, to call it original is to give it more than its due since—like many another Deep Purple number (see above)—it is a near-actionable rip-off of another song, in this case, Hendrix's 'Foxy Lady'.

It has also been said that it borrows much from something called 'Lost Soul' by one Bill Parkinson, a performance of which can be found on YouTube. Since, however, the video seems to be of recent vintage, the accusations of plagiarism aimed at Deep Purple are, in this instance, less easy to verify, despite Parkinson's claim to have been paid off to keep quiet. Regardless of such controversies, 'Mandrake Root' remains a heavy riff-led piece that outlived Mark I as a staple of the band's live sets into the Mark II era, turning into a vehicle for weird and wonderful improvisations that would often last for half an hour or more.

Of all the tracks on Shades of Deep Purple, 'Mandrake Root' is the one that most comes across as the work of an embryonic hard rock combo. In hindsight, it can also be seen as the battleground of different musical impulses within the band and a record of diverse talents struggling for full compatibility. The riff has been credited to Blackmore and it suggests strongly that, even at this early stage, he had ideas about steering the band in a heavier direction. Lord's contribution, too, has a power lacking elsewhere. Evans, by contrast, sounds uncomfortable, his croony voice at odds with a backing upon which it fails to impose any real authority.

It would take Ian Gillan, in later live takes on the song, to bring out the full force of the vocal part, his screaming delivery matching the aural mayhem against which it was pitted.

Back in the present, my trips to The Record Shop and Slough had got me started, but I was aware that they did not amount to much material progress. Rod Evans was still an elusive spectre. At least, though, the quest was up and running...

Adrian Jarvis

3—And The Address

WHERE DO YOU start to look for a recluse? In this day and age, the answer to that one's simple: on the Internet. As useful as the World Wide Web is, though, I can't help feeling sometimes that it takes much of the romance and adventure out of life.

Perhaps that's why it's very difficult to imagine an Indiana Jones existing in the twenty-first century. Frankly, he would have nothing to do; why go off to Tibet and Egypt and God-knows-where-else in search of the Ark of the Covenant when there's probably a blog or forum online that can tell you exactly where it is and why it's less interesting than the Holy Grail (available from www.callthatagrailthisisagrail.com) ?

In my own small way I had started this quest all those years earlier as a minor Indiana Jones flipping through the empty LP covers in the racks of Lotus Records. But that world has gone forever; the first place to go with any piece of research now is the iMAC in my kitchen at which I customarily sit with, depending on the time of day, a coffee or a glass of wine or a whisky in my hand. I accessed the (admittedly rather Indiana Jonesish sounding) programme 'Safari' and entered 'Where is Rod Evans of Deep Purple?' into its search box.

The first thing that struck me was just how few results were returned. Actually, over two million results were returned, but hardly any of them expressed any curiosity about Evans' current whereabouts. For the most part, what I got were links to historical documents about his time in Deep Purple, together with old interviews and so on—none of which were any help at all. The band's official website carried a strand which was promisingly titled 'Where is Rod Evans, Now?' Unfortunately, its most recent entry was from four years previously and the single page of comments contained little of interest and certainly nothing that could offer much of a clue.

An article on the unofficial, but highly authoritative, Deep Purple fan website The Highway Star called 'Mission: Impossible' seemed to promise even less than this, since it dated back all the way to 2006 and had apparently long-since fizzled out. The writer had essentially put in motion a quest much like the one upon which I was engaged; he challenged the website's readers to search for the elusive Evans and to post their findings as comments to his piece. Discouragingly, the number of responses was meagre—to say the least—but there were some enticing titbits. A mysterious contributor with the username 'Fan' seemed to know more than he was letting on, hinting that, in line with the rumours that had been flying around for years, Evans was working as a doctor or paramedic in California.

As long ago as 1978, Jon Lord, speaking to the Belgian Deep Purple Fan Club (yes, there is one) talked about this, saying:

> *Rod's a paramedic in Los Angeles. It's a very brave job. It's a very good social service. He goes out...the doctors go out with the police when they have an emergency or a shooting. He's one of those. He was raising German Shepherds for a while, training them. He divorced, got married again and the girl he married was a nurse and he got interested and became a paramedic. He went to school for it and that's what he's doing now.*

On a rather dark note, there was a suggestion that Evans' licence to practice carried some sort of endorsement as a result of a conviction for drunk driving. Excitingly, though, 'Fan' supplied some hypertext links that appeared to be the gateways to real breakthroughs, but, frustratingly, one of them led to an expired page and another was to a website called Zaba Search that listed literally hundreds of Rod and Rodney Evanses living in California, providing too little information on any of them for a definite identification to be made—and that's assuming that Rod Evans still went by the name 'Rod Evans'....

As another contributor to The Highway Star piece, one 'Fan 2', huffily wrote:

> ...*sorry but you guys have not found him. thanks for all the useless info' [sic].*

I should have expected no more than this. After all, if finding Rod Evans were that easy, it would have been accomplished years ago. 'Fan' did make one interesting suggestion, though, which was to contact Thames Talent, Deep Purple's management that (he thought) had represented Evans during his singing career. It seemed worth following up.

Another lead came from Evans' Wikipedia entry. This ended by reporting a rumour that Evans had been contacted by Larry 'Rhino' Reinhardt, the guitarist with Captain Beyond about a possible reunion, but had declined to be involved. If, then, I could find Reinhardt, I could try to set up an interview in which it might be possible to learn something of Evans' current location....

I put Reinhardt's name into Wikipedia. He had died three months earlier. This was typical of the luck that I was having.

While this was all very disappointing, it did put certain matters into perspective. It should, perhaps, have come as little surprise that my initial Safari search had come up short, but it was odd that sites specifically devoted to Deep Purple and their history had so little to say on the subject of Evans' whereabouts. Those couple of half-hearted appeals for input from the fans was as far as it went—and the appeals had clearly elicited little but apathy. I wondered if the main reason for Evans' continued post-Purple obscurity was merely that no-one really cared where he was?

That, then, was my job: to care.

Reinvigorated with a new sense of mission by this realisation, I decided to take up Fan's suggestions by getting in touch with Thames Talent—based in Connecticut—and ask if they had any contact details for Rod Evans. Given that this resolution came to me late at night, I opted for email as the best way to strike while the iron was hot.

But sending an email proved to be easier said than done.

My assumption was that the agency would have an internet homepage on which there would be an email address to which I could send a message (futile—probably) asking for help. No such thing existed. There were plenty of those business directory pages that listed the company, giving the address of the office, a phone number and even the information that the company's owner was Bruce Payne—a name I had come across in much Purple-related literature—but no email address. I continued to search with an increasing sense of annoyance.

Finally, by dropping the reference to Connecticut from my Google search, I came up with...a web page with the word 'Thames' at the top of it in curly writing. And nothing else.

By some circuitous Google-led route, I found myself on the official Deep Purple website typing the following into its contact form:

> *Hi! I am trying to locate Rod Evans for some research that I am doing and the best lead I have received so far is to contact Thames Talent—I cannot, however, find an email address for that company. I wonder, then, if you either: know where Rod Evans is (unlikely) or could give me a contact email address for Thames Talent? Whatever help you can give would be much appreciated...*

At last, I felt like I was getting somewhere. Unfortunately, before I could send the email I had to fill in one of those box things where you look at some letters and numbers that have been printed in a weird way and re-type them in Times New Roman. Now this should not have caused me much of a problem, especially given how easy these particular versions of this puzzle were, but I simply could not get the damn thing to accept my answers. I was sure that I was not missing anything out, but the form kept coming back, inviting me to fill in the meaningless little combinations of symbols over and over again.

In the end, I gave up, feeling like fate was deliberately working against me. Quite why I had been so singled out for so much bad luck, I could not have begun to imagine; after all, I was only trying to find a washed-up old rock and roller, not alter the fundamental laws of the universe.

I was beginning to come to the conclusion that this could well be a quest without a discovery and, more worryingly, a book without a climax.

What was Plan B? I decided to go for broke.

I decided that I would attempt to contact Simon Robinson.

For those who don't know, Simon Robinson is essentially Mr. Deep Purple. It is he who runs the grandiosely titled Deep Purple Appreciation Society (DPAS), he who managed the band's back catalogue and the remastered releases to which it occasionally gives rise, he who writes the notes for the CD inlay cards and he who was largely responsible for reviving the Purple Records label under which the band's later seventies releases had first been issued. If anyone could help with the quest to find Rod Evans, it would be him. It seemed that the only way to accomplish this was to email him through the DPAS website, so I sent him the following:

Rod Evans: so WHERE is he? I am doing a bit of research for my own satisfaction (although I would be happy to share any findings I might make—but don't hold your breath on this as yet...) and would be interested in acquiring any material you might have of relevance. Obviously, if any of it is in a commercial form, I will buy it!

Perhaps the society's members could be mobilised in this search—although I see that a different website has already attempted this with a notable lack of success. Anyway, I look forward to hearing from you...

Again, I had no idea what, if anything, to expect. What I got was a reply—almost immediately:

I managed to reach some of his old band mates and a couple of them keep in touch amazingly enough. We'd ideally like to get some finance to offer Rod a fee to be interviewed properly, I can't see him wanting to do it otherwise!
—Simon

This was a major breakthrough! In a state of almost febrile excitement, I replied with:

Hi Simon! Bloody hell! How much do you think he would ask for? I would have thought that, within reason, we could get together a fee that he would find acceptable (I have some friends with a few quid and, hey, provided that he doesn't ask for silly money, I could chip in a bit myself). I would love to talk to him. Do you have the contact details of the band members who are still in touch with him? Just to fill you in on my own credentials, I am a genuine researcher—I've even got a certificate to prove it!—and I am used to interviewing people, so I think that I could get some home truths out of Rod...if only we can find him...

Simon had given me one idea. I got on to good old Wikipedia and found out the names of Evans' Captain Beyond band mates. The first that was mentioned was that of Bobby Caldwell, the drummer. Like most old rockers, he had an official site, so I accessed it and, again like most old rockers, it included a facility for contacting him (it might be the best thing about the formerly famous that they are so easy to reach). I sent the following email:

> Hi Bobby!
> I've been doing a bit of research into the current whereabouts of Rod Evans. I know that you played with him in the early seventies—those early Captain Beyond songs are really excellent and certainly deserve more airplay than they get. Perhaps finding Rod would allow them to be brought to the fore again (after all, I'm pretty sure that the musical press would be interested to learn that Rod had been contacted). What I'm asking, then, is if you are still in touch with Rod? If so, do you think that he would be prepared to be contacted and interviewed? I would really appreciate any help that you could give with this.
> With thanks for any help that you can give.

Nothing came of this and things were beginning to lose momentum again. Then, Simon replied, placing the following in my inbox:

> I've no idea what to offer him, but will tackle that if we get through. I wish I had more time to indulge in this, we found their first roadie a couple of years ago but being in America I never got around to calling for a chat.

I was slightly troubled by this one, to be honest. What was I to make of that word 'indulge'? Was there a tetchy tone to it, as though Simon could not really be bothered and was unhappy that I kept bringing it up? It was possible, but, then, I had not exactly bombarded him with email after email; if he had wanted to ignore me, it would have been relatively easy to do so. Reckoning on balance that he was happy to engage in constructive dialogue, I wrote a reply:

> *Hi Simon!*
> *Sorry to keep bringing this up (!), but would you happen to still have the contact details for that roadie? I can try to call him or send him an email (hey! you never know, he might even be on Facebook...)*
> > *Cheers!*

The reply duly came back:

> *Let me dig through my old paperwork for you. In the meantime I've remembered his name, Mick Angus. He saw the advert, applied to be Mk 1 singer, went back and told his mate Rod Evans, who promptly went for an audition himself and got the job! As they felt sorry for Mick they gave him a job as roadie.*

A name! It was possible that Simon would get back to me with the details I had requested, but I decided that I would be a bit more pro-active than simply to wait. I set to work trying to find Mick Angus.

There was little to go on. The Internet provided me with almost nothing. The name popped up in articles about the early years of Deep Purple—mostly to confirm what Simon had told me in his email—and, occasionally, in the context of a technical credit that its owner supposedly received for the album Deep Purple In Rock, although a quick scan of the inlay card to my CD copy (liner notes by Simon Robinson) failed to confirm this.

There was one straw to grasp at: it seemed that Angus had

appeared in Florida, several months earlier, at an event featured on the website Meetup (total attendance: five) centred around a band called Nobody's Darlings. If, then, they had contact details for Mick, I could…and then… it was, at least, intriguing…I joined the site and sent the following to whom it may have concerned:

> *Hi!*
>
> *I notice that Mick Angus, the former Deep Purple roadie, attended your event on October 14, 2011 9:30 PM, featuring Nobody's Darlings. I am keen to get in touch with Mick (not for any dodgy purpose—I am researching early Deep Purple and would love to hear his views on certain matters); do you happen to have contact details for him (ideally, an email address)? I would be very grateful if you could supply me with any information that you might have.*

Once again, all I could do was sit back and wait…

Nothing came back, so I accessed the Nobody's Darlings MySpace page and sent the following email:

> *Hi!*
>
> *According to MeetUp, the former Deep Purple roadie, Mick Angus, attended an event featuring yourselves on October 14th 2011. I wonder if you happen to have contact details for Mick (I am doing a bit of research to which he may be able to contribute)? Ideally, I would get an email address, but a phone number would be equally useful (I live in England). I appreciate any help you may be able to give.*

While awaiting a reply (if such was going to be forthcoming), I went back to the one element in all of this that was absolutely certain, the music. I accessed iTunes and took myself on a journey through Mark I's recordings. Shades of Deep Purple had come and gone and now I turned to the second release, The Book of Taliesyn.

The cover to this one is the most bizarre in Purple history. Credited to John Vernon Lord (no relation to the band's keyboard player), it is a perspective-free fantasy of medieval minstrels and strange, gothic castles. Ships sail in the distance past islands linked by wooden causeways. A hare leaps over a fish. A bird flies—or perhaps it's swooping. A chess board with only one set of pieces dominates what foreground there is. Cone-like lines curve around and cross through the scene, perhaps in imitation of musical sounds, flowing in the air.

The band's name and the title of the album appear several times in different places and the names of Mark I's personnel—but only their first names—are listed, along with their individual skill sets. The picture's pen-and-ink lines, hand-drawn lettering and flat tints are somehow wholly characteristic of the time in which it was produced.

Quite what it all means is open to debate, but a clue comes from the title, which is a reference to a collection of poems attributed to an eighth century Welsh bard best known for his contributions to the Arthurian mythos. What can be said is that, as a cover, it is a considerable improvement on the poor effort that first meets any prospective purchaser of 'Shades'—as I and the owner of The Record Shop had agreed.

The mystical imagery continues in the first song, an original called 'Listen, Learn, Read On' the lyrics of which enjoin the listener to do all three of those things to the Book of Taliesyn itself. The song's staccato, fuzz box-infused riff immediately announces that a harder edge has come into the band's sound. The spoken verses are an experiment that would not previously have been dared and actually anticipate the 'talking blues' style that Ian Gillan would put to successful use on Mark II numbers like 'No One Came'.

As an opening, 'Listen, Learn, Read On' is a notable statement of intent that suggests the band was restless to move into more original territory than had been the case with their debut.

That said, there are still several cover versions, the eclecticism of which again makes the location of any specific Purple 'core' difficult. There is the inevitable slowed-down Beatles song, this time 'We Can Work It Out', which is interesting only because it is preceded by another of those newly-composed preludes that have an air of abandon missing from the song itself.

The run-through of 'Kentucky Woman'—which was released as a single—has a certain kitsch charm that has endeared it to fans. It proved popular enough for there to be extant recordings of the Mark II line-up performing it live. But—really—it's a Neil Diamond song: was this ever the right direction for a band of Purple's sensibility? As for 'River Deep, Mountain High'—with a musical prologue that includes snatches of Strauss's 'Also Sprach Zarathustra' and a ten-minute running time, this seems to have been conceived as the album's centrepiece. It isn't.

It's one of those strange facts about the sixties that bands would often cover songs that had only been written and first recorded in the recent past. Today this would be most unlikely to happen—odd exceptions such as Amy Winehouse releasing a version of The Zutons' 'Valerie' aside. A reasonable interval would now be expected—and left—between a song's first appearance and its cover by a different artist.

This is true even of sampling, the process by which snippets of older songs are used within a more-or-less original composition, as, for example, when the riff to Tubeway Army's 'Are Friends Electric?' found its way into the otherwise totally different 'Freak Like Me' by Sugababes.

In the sixties, though, it seems that, once a song was out there, it was regarded as a generally exploitable resource. All of Mark I Deep Purple's cover versions are of songs that had only recently been hits for other people. Even 'Hush' had been in the Billboard Hot 100 for Billy Joe Royal less than a year before Deep Purple made it their own.

Equally odd was the stylistic range of the cover versions that bands chose to do. Given Deep Purple's rock orientation, numbers by the Beatles, Ike and Tina Turner and, of all people, Neil Diamond would not have seemed like obvious choices and, yet, there they are, loud and proud, rubbing shoulders with each other as well as the band's own compositions.

What this tells us about the music industry at the time is not easy to say, beyond the bland statement that it clearly indicates considerable evolution and refinement of record companies' marketing strategies since then. It might also be pointed out that, in that 'pop' music as such had only been around for a decade or so, it was not surprising that a cover version would be of a relatively new song. In Deep Purple's case, it perhaps demonstrates how hard the band was finding it to pin down an identity and a direction. The Vanilla Fudge influences are less evident in The Book of Taliesyn than they are on 'Shades', but there seemed to be little consensus as to what might replace them.

Nevertheless, it is as a record of the band's growing confidence as songwriters that 'Taliesyn' is most interesting. All of the new numbers are winners on some level. 'Wring That Neck' is a classic instrumental that, like 'Mandrake Root', remained an epic set list staple well into the Mark II era. 'Shield' is rather pompous lyrically, but is sufficiently complex musically to have earned it the status in some critics' eyes of 'Mark's I's Masterpiece'. I would not agree with that but it cannot be denied that it represents considerable progress over anything to be found on the debut album.

Of all the songs on 'Taliesyn', it is 'Anthem' that, in retrospect, merits most discussion. Starting off with a little gentle acoustic guitar, it moves into some ballady crooning from Evans, before a church-organ-like solo from Lord takes the song into an instrumental section that sees the band trading licks with a string backing. The interplay between the rocky solos of the band and the more classical cadences of the string players is surprisingly effective and skilfully done.

What the song showcases is a certain schizophrenia in the band that was to cause considerable tensions between the players and almost lead to what would have been a terminal schism. As 'Anthem' demonstrates, two directions lay open to the band in late 1968: they could either become art rockers, carrying out esoteric musical experiments with orchestras and other ensembles to a small, but well-informed, audience, or they could go for the big prize of hard rock fame and fortune.

'Taliesyn' is the opening of that debate—one that was never resolved by Mark I. It took the double-header of the 'Concerto For Group and Orchestra' and Mark II's first studio product, 'In Rock', for the matter to be settled in favour of rock 'n' roll. This was also the moment that musical leadership in the band passed from Jon Lord to Ritchie Blackmore—where it remained, either in actuality or in influence, until the end of the band's career.

It was thinking about the whole history of the band that led to me visiting YouTube to re-watch that 'Rock Family Trees' episode from the mid-90s on Deep Purple. I noticed that it was produced by one Francis Hanly and, a short internet search later, I had his current work email address, so, in the shit-or-bust-nothing-to-lose frame of mind that my internet searches had put me into, I sent him the following—more in hope than expectation:

> *Hi Francis!*
> *I don't need to tell you that you produced the Rock Family Trees series, oh, quite a long time ago now and, again, I really don't need to tell you that one of the programmes was about Deep Purple. Well, I am doing a little research into the elusive Rod Evans and, more specifically, his current whereabouts and think that you might be able to help. I know that Rod did not appear on the programme, but is there the slightest chance that you, or one of your researchers, may have obtained contact*

details for him? I appreciate that we are going back some
way here and that, even if the answer is "yes", such details
may no longer be accurate, but, even so, any hint would
be useful. I have been in contact with some of the people
who worked with Rod and, so far, have drawn a blank, so
this is not the easiest piece of research which I have ever
undertaken—although, if it yields some results, there
could be an interesting programme in it...

Whatever else I discovered on this quest, I came to realize that, on the whole, people are willing to help out if they can, because a reply came back almost within the hour:

One of my all time favourites to make but sadly we got no
closer to Rod than you. Had we got a lead we would have
pursued it as I think he's fascinating. Good luck with your
search!
Best, Francis

This was hugely discouraging. If the resources available to the BBC—full-time researchers, industry contacts, a global network of offices and correspondents—had failed to unearth any clues as to Rod Evans' location, what hope did I, an independent researcher on a limited budget, have?

Still, at least I had finally got the Deep Purple website contact page to work and had sent my email asking for an address or phone number for Thames Talent. An answer came back pretty quickly— from an exotically named female:

Well, as I work for Thames Talent you will have to do
with me. Last I heard he was somewhere in California.
That's pretty much it.

That was a bit brusque, I thought. But its very peremptoriness suggested that I might be heading down the wrong track. What, though, was the right track?

At that moment, the only 'tracks' I had were the songs on the albums, so I went back to my musical explorations and put on the third album, the one simply entitled Deep Purple or, as my MP3 Player would have it 'Deep Purple III'.

As an album, it tends not to be well regarded by critics and fans alike. This is strange since, of all of Mark I's output, it is the one that best showcases something like a specific Purple style.

Cover versions this time out are restricted to a token one, Donovan's 'Lalena', which is competently done, if unremarkable. Otherwise, this is an album of new material. Appropriately, one track—another instrumental 'prologue' to a song—is called 'Fault Line' which more-or-less sums up the musical tensions to which the album bears witness. On the plus side, those very tensions make 'Deep Purple' arguably the most experimental album that the band has ever produced. Less positively, they describe an unsustainable situation that was to see some political legerdemain leading to a coup d'etat at the end of which Evans and Simper were sacked in what can only be called (using yet more French) a fait accomplit.

Opener 'Chasing Shadows' gets things off to a fast-moving start. Experimentation is to the fore here, the track being essentially a chance for Ian Paice to indulge himself with every percussive instrument he can lay his hands on.

'Blind' comes next. This is supposedly a love song, although that is not obvious from the lyrics. Again, the emphasis is on the unusual, the main instrument being—of all things—a harpsichord, Blackmore's guitar being relegated to the background.

Then comes 'Lalena', after which we get the diptych of 'Fault Line' and 'The Painter'. The former makes extensive use of back-tracking—a psychedelic touch. The latter is the first indication on the album of where the band would go once the bloodletting that ended Mark I was over. Neither the riff nor the organ part nor the funky rhythm would sound out of place on a Mark II (or even Mark

III) track. While not particularly special in its own right, 'The Painter' is important for what it says about the development of the band's sound.

Something similar could be said for 'Why Didn't Rosemary' which is another pacey rocker, albeit one that takes its template from twelve bar blues. I have never understood why this song is not more popular. Heavy and drily humorous, it is a solid slice of entertainment that showcases Blackmore, in particular, at his best.

Pretension is back in 'Bird Has Flown'. This is a re-draft of a song, 'The Bird Has Flown', that had previously been released on a single (the dropping of the 'the' is significant—apparently). It is an object lesson in leaving well alone. The earlier version is vastly superior, being driven by a chugging guitar riff and some relentless drumming. For the more leanly-titled album run-through, the band decided to overlay everything with an intrusive wah-wah guitar track and end with an anti-climactic organ solo.

Which leads on to 'April'. At over twelve minutes, it is the longest studio recording the band has ever produced. On the album's liner notes, it is described as 'a sort of three part concert about the month of April'. While the use of the word 'concert' here is jarring—why not 'song'?—it pretty much sums the track up.

Part one is basically a duet for Blackmore, playing both acoustic and electric guitars, and Lord, who does a little twee organ soloing. A few choral 'aaahs' are stuck somewhere in the mix, but the whole thing could be the soundtrack of a grainy documentary lamenting the loss to modernisation of some folky craft or other.

Abruptly, the track goes into part two which is Jon Lord's orchestral description of April. As enjoyable as this is on its own terms, it is, when all is said and done, several minutes of a Deep Purple album to which no member of Deep Purple contributes a thing. Part three is the electrified and amped up bit. The liner notes tell us that this is a treatment of section one in a 'more Purple way', an odd statement coming from a band that had yet to find its musical identity. Actually, it sounds not unlike 'The Painter' and is the only part of the full track on which all members of the band, including Rod Evans, play.

In that it represents a continuation of Lord's attempts to reconcile rock and classical, 'April' is not to be dismissed and it certainly anticipates the 'Concerto or Group and Orchestra'. However, by keeping the orchestral and band sections separate, it is less successful than its illustrious successor, or, for that matter, the earlier 'Anthem'.

It is perhaps a symptom of the furious pace of recording that 'April' does not sound like a more finished product. To produce three albums in little more than a year—as Mark I had done—was a feat that would be unheard of today. What it did allow was a fairly speedy assessment of where the band was going. On listening to the albums back-to-back it should be obvious to anyone that the answer would be 'nowhere very clear'. Musical power struggles were only half of the issue. The truth is that the biggest problem was the presence at the front of the stage of that man, Rod Evans.

Films of him singing with the band indicate that whatever charisma he possessed would have been more suited to a light, poppy ensemble than the rock juggernaut that seemed to have been forming in Ritchie Blackmore's imagination. More serious was the problem of his voice. It's not that he could not sing; his deep croon suited a certain sixties style and, when paired with a backing that matched it—as on, for example, 'Shield' or 'Hush'—it worked very well. But it simply could not cope with heavier songs and often sounded strained when attempting to deal with the uncompromising power of a 'Mandrake Root' or a 'Why Didn't Rosemary'.

Neither are Evans' lyrics as excellent as they are sometimes said to be. Ian Gillan would later go on to prove himself a quirky and intelligent writer whose contributions to Purple songs— although spoken of modestly by the singer himself—are a significant part of their effect. 'Strange Kind of Woman', for example, tells the story of a loser's infatuation with a prostitute, his passion only being requited at the point of her death. 'Anyone's Daughter' is equally amusing, again being a narrative about a man who, unlucky in love, marries a 'rich man's daughter' more by good luck than judgement.

Gillan's protest songs also merit a mention. 'Child in Time' is only one example; there is genuine anger in 'Mary Long' and a sense of loss in a later-career piece like 'Fingers to the Bone'.

Moreover, he has consistently shown a real facility with language. The famous line from 'Smoke on the Water' concerning the 'Rolling truck Stones thing' is only the most obvious case in point.

His nonsense songs—at least one of which can be found on most Deep Purple albums—are packed with puns, assonance and internal rhymes. In 'Speed King' we get 'tooty fruity was, oh, so rooty', while 'Space Truckin'' includes some wonderfully pointless imagery, such as, 'we've got music in our solar system' and 'we danced around the Borealis'.

Rod Evans' lyrics never approached this level of wit although they could be quite erudite and literary. The references to 'The Book of Taliesyn' in 'Listen, Learn, Read On' demonstrate a good breadth of reading, while 'Why Didn't Rosemary' takes its cues from the Roman Polanski film 'Rosemary's Baby' in which Mia Farrow gives birth to the Anti-Christ (the question being asked—very topically for the sixties—is 'why didn't Rosemary ever take the pill?'). The first line of 'April' ('April is a cruel time') can only be a reference to T. S. Eliot's 'The Waste Land'.

Being scholarly, though, does not necessarily make the lyrics fun and too many of Evans' songs are over-serious and more than a little pompous. Even in the sixties, much of his imagery must have sounded arcane and unworldly. Take 'Bird Has Flown' which starts with:

Oh, the beggar on his cornerstone

Catches pity in his wrinkled hand...

...before going on to...

All the children in the distant house
They have feelings only children know'.

The 'distant house' is evocative, but what are these special infantile feelings? As much as the image of 'catching pity' has some genuine poetic force to it, it is a little outweighed by the question of what on earth is a 'cornerstone' and in what ways one might be associated with beggars? There is also something lip-curlingly fay about 'The Painter': 'Writer, Make me up a play, Writer, Make the meaning gay'.

Jon Lord has spoken about how the group could have been 'braver and nicer' about how they moved Evans and Simper out and brought Gillan and Glover in. Notoriously, the new boys were already writing and recording with the core trio before their predecessors had been informed of their fate.

Yes, it could have been handled better, but it is difficult to regret the fact of it happening at all—albeit that Simper was an innocent and undeserving victim. Deep Purple Mark I never found its feet. There were memorable moments, some promising songs and, in 'Hush', one indelible classic, but the sound was just too unfocused, the experiments too ambitious, the talents involved too diverse.

Where the band might have gone after the Third Album can only be imagined.

More of the same? A brief career working with orchestras before the whole thing's inevitable implosion? Whatever the merits of the music, the signs of progress are weak. With the benefit of hindsight, it can be seen that the band desperately needed the injection of creativity that came with the recruitment of Gillan and Glover.

And so Rod Evans departed for newer pastures. His career in rock was not over and he continued to work with other musicians for some time to come. Moreover, he may have left Deep Purple for good but he was not yet done with 'Deep Purple'.

The most bizarre, and, for our purposes, significant, episode in his association with that name still lay in his future.

4—Hey Bop a Re Bop

IT COULD HAVE been a room in any relatively small house on a modern suburban estate. Three piece suite. Television. Curvy legged dining table table in the corner at which I sat with Jerry Bloom, publisher, author and fellow hardcore Deep Purple fan. Even the large collection of vinyl records stacked under and around the hi-fi separates system was not especially unusual, although it was the first clue that we were in a house of rock and roll.

No, you had to look harder.

At the square, empty bottle on the sideboard, engraved with a personalized 'thank you' message for taking part in a successful Scandinavian tour. At the test pressings of what are now regarded as classics hidden amongst those densely packed twelve inch LPs. Above all, at the gold disc of Deep Purple's 'Stormbringer' album displayed on the wall.

Jerry and I were there to meet Ian Hansford, whose home it was. Hansford was a former roadie who, like the elusive Mick Angus, had worked with Deep Purple from their foundation, his involvement taking him right up to the dying days of Mark II. He was tall, very thin and sported a thick plume of pure white hair that, although cut relatively short, looked like its natural state was to reach somewhere below his shoulders. He had clearly once been a man not to be trifled with; indeed, his nickname, 'Bige', alluded to his size. The reduced state in which we found him was the only outward sign of the stroke that he had suffered and to which he frequently referred. I had been introduced to him by Jerry, who correctly surmised that he might be a source of some interesting stories about Mark I in general and Rod Evans in particular.

Over two fascinating hours, Hansford took us through a small history of late sixties and early seventies rock and roll, mentioning virtually everyone of any note from that era, most of whom he had known personally. Some of what he said was relevant to my quest, some of it was just of interest in its own right, but all of it was worth listening to.

For example, he told us about a night in a hotel on New York's Fifth Avenue when he and Evans, having been invited to a wealthy guest's party, found themselves accosted by someone, perhaps the host, who took exception to such a pair of 'long haired freaks'. Evans' response was to throw his drink in the man's face. Only the swift intervention of Hansford himself prevented Evans from being beaten up by the man's burly minders. It was behaviour that Hansford described as untypical, Evans, he said, generally being quite a calm and collected person.

Hansford's take on the end of Mark I was particularly enlightening. He said that Evans, 'had visions of being a movie star', but was uncertain as to 'what went wrong' with that ambition.

I suggested that maybe Evans couldn't act.

'It was downhill,' Hansford said, 'It was downhill after that. I don't think he was putting the effort in. He wasn't creating much. There wasn't a lot of input from him and I think, in the end, it must have shown through to the other people involved and they said, "He's not putting in, he's just turning up, he's not putting a lot of effort in and his mind's somewhere else," and I think they decided that it was time for him to go.'

Post-Purple, Evans joined Captain Beyond whose output I had been attempting to source at The Record Shop and whose surviving members I had been trying to contact. Interestingly, Wikipedia describes them as American, it coming as news to me that Slough is in America. But that, in itself, tells us something about Evans' mindset at the time. He seems increasingly to have identified more closely with the USA than his own country. Apart from Evans, Captain Beyond consisted of past members of other Purple-like outfits such as Iron Butterfly.

They need not detain us for long. Their niche in rock history is small to say the least, although their music can still be obtained from Amazon. What it sounds like is—well, Deep Purple, to be honest. And not Mark I, either. The riffs would not be out of place on a Mark II album. That is not to say, however, that it is derivative or easily dismissed. To my surprise, when I got listening to Captain Beyond as part of this quest, I liked what I heard.

There is a relentlessness to the music that even an uncompromising aural onslaught like Deep Purple In Rock would struggle to equal. The songs have a genuine sense of abandon to them, the heavy riffs pounding away in mesmeric patterns (perhaps showing the Iron Butterfly influence). It certainly has to be said that a piece like 'Dancing Madly Backwards' deserves more respect than it gets.

Again, though, Evans is the cog that doesn't quite turn. He generally achieves a power on Captain Beyond tracks that his contributions to Deep Purple lack, but that still does not elevate him into the pantheon of great rock vocalists. It's hard to imagine him screaming—but that is just what Captain Beyond's songs need him to do. There is a restraint to his singing that sits uneasily with its, often insane, backing.

To be fair, it is to be wondered if Evans himself was coming around to this opinion. His tenure with Captain Beyond lasted for just two albums. Perhaps he himself could see that he was not the right person to belt out anthemic chunks of hard rock. As Ian Hansford told me, Evans' interest in being with Deep Purple waned towards the end of his stint with the band (Nick Simper has also said as much in interviews); it would seem that he was not completely the put-upon innocent in his eventual removal. Did something similar happen with Captain Beyond?

Evans was beginning to transform in my mind into something of a rock dilettante.

The same could not be said of his fellow Mark I refugee Nick Simper who tried to keep a professional musical career alive as Deep Purple faded into his past. After a couple of short-lived false starts, he formed a band called Warhorse that toured and recorded for a period in the early seventies. Rather less glamorous than the would-be 'supergroup' that was Captain Beyond, Warhorse largely stuck to the Deep Purple Mark I template, producing songs that were quite heavy without ever getting into the realms of what most people would recognise as hard rock.

They were also derivative to a degree that even those inveterate cultural magpies Deep Purple themselves would have baulked at, although there is some poetic justice in the chief source of Warhorse's plundering being Deep Purple's back catalogue. The song 'Burning', for example, begins with a lead-in that is a dead ringer for one of 'Child in Time's instrumental breaks before settling into a riff that is suspiciously similar to that of 'Bird Has Flown', while 'Ritual' is so close to 'Wring That Neck' as to be virtually a vocal version of it.

None of this, of course, would be a problem if the songs were inspired in other ways. The playing is excellent, but there is just too much going on: any given Warhorse song sounds like it contains more riffs than every Deep Purple album up to and including In Rock combined. The public at the time were just as unconvinced as I am. Although they gigged diligently, the band failed to make much headway and, when their singles and albums left the charts untroubled, their record label decided that enough was enough and cut them adrift.

What happened to Simper subsequently only becomes relevant at the point at which he wound up in The Good Old Boys. Essentially a bit of fun, The Boys' MySpace page rather grandiosely describes the band as a side-project for its members between other gigs. There is no doubt that the band's members are accomplished musicians, most having been in a range of sixties and seventies groups from Deep Purple (obviously), to Warhorse, The Strawbs and Renaissance.

Simper also worked with Nasty Habits, an Austrian Deep Purple tribute act that concentrated on the Mark I era, for whom he played a 'very special guest' role. Well-meaning, but of routine competence, Nasty Habits were mostly notable for the zeal with which they trotted out songs that had not seen the light of day for decades and, in some cases, not at all outside of a studio, often, it must be said, for very good reasons. Still, who can begrudge Simper his chance to finally profit a little from material that he mostly co-wrote and which has never been unavailable for all the fact that it did not achieve the fame of the output of later Deep Purple marks?

Having taken the tentative step of beginning my quest by looking for old vinyl copies of Mark I's albums at The Record Shop and gone in search of Rod Evans' childhood home, I decided that the next step would be to see The Good Old Boys in concert and—who knows—maybe take the opportunity to buttonhole Nick Simper and ask him a few questions about his Deep Purple experience and some of the people with whom he shared it.

Of course, there are plenty of interviews with Simper available which probably contain everything he knows about his time with the band. But that is not quite the same as actually speaking to someone and, since access to him did not seem to be particularly difficult to arrange, I thought it would be useful to give it a go.

In preparing this picaresque little tale, I had been spending a fair bit of time on Nick Simper's admirable website. Cheekily, I left the following message on his message board:

> Hi Nick! I am a massive fan of Deep Purple and have been for thirty-odd years now. I particularly enjoy Mark I and, in fact, am doing a bit of research into them at the moment. I would love to get your views on a few things. I guess you must get similar requests a lot, but my email

address is there for you to see if you have time to get in touch.

I must admit that my expectations were not high, but—what the hell!—you have to try; the buttonhole-at-a-gig option was always a viable Plan B...

And a gig came up. I was searching through The Good Old Boys' MySpace page when I chanced on a list of forthcoming engagements and there was one I could easily get to—in the rather unglamorous town of Nuneaton in the West Midlands. At a sports and social club. At a cost of £4 to non-members.

Now Nuneaton may like to tout itself as the original for George Eliot's Middlemarch, but it is not exactly the sort of place that Nick Simper must have pictured himself playing when he was rubbing shoulders with Hugh Hefner on Playboy TV all those years earlier. In some respects, it did represent a measure of progress in that most Good Old Boys gigs took place in and around Uxbridge near London—which, presumably, is close to the homes of some or all of them. Nuneaton, then, was almost a stop on a wide-ranging tour. It was certainly a reminder that showbiz is a fickle mistress and that even someone, like Simper (who could still boast an international fan base) can find himself having to wrestle with humility if he wishes to keep on working.

Karen and I set off from her house in Nottingham at 6:45 for the journey that Multimap had informed us would take around 55 minutes. It was glorious weather, the sort that turns the English countryside into Planet Earth's one indisputable masterpiece of miniaturist design. The fields, hedges and forests of the Midlands slipped picturesquely past us as we followed the motorway from east to west. It was strange to think that we were going to a rock and roll gig; a real ale festival or country fayre would have better fitted the scenery.

We arrived at the Sports and Social Club in what was still broad daylight. The place was not actually in Nuneaton, but stood next to a field through which a public footpath curved away into a distance cut off from our view by a line of trees.

We left Karen's Citroën on the stony piece of scrubland that served as a car park and, both of us feeling unaccountably nervous, headed towards what I hoped would be a meeting with a legend, or, anyway, someone I regarded as a legend. As we walked in, we passed a number of sullen looking youngsters who were huddled in a covered smoking area holding a séance with the acrid ghosts that their cigarettes had summoned up. The club building lay just beyond them. It was a low rise, grey concrete pile with an uninviting entrance of the type that you might find on a 1970s-vintage primary school.

Inside, the clubroom was large and nondescript. On both sides there were long banquettes in functional and uncomfortable beige in front of which were two lines of basic, unfussy tables. More tables and chairs were arranged in little islands around the room. The place looked like it would serve better as the setting for an old folks' beetle drive than a rock and roll gig.

Karen bought us a beer each from the bar in the corner and we settled down on a part of the banquette towards the back of the room, still conscious of our status as non-members and, therefore, in some obscure way, interlopers. There was hardly anybody else there. I counted twenty people, most of whom seemed to be pensioners; they would have been young—or relatively young—when Deep Purple Mark I were at their height.

The stage was set in a corner diagonally opposite from Karen and me. It was low and narrow and almost completely taken up with the drum kit that was already in place. Behind it on the wall were two spangly curtains that may or may not have been put there specifically for the occasion. A couple of old guys, one wearing a cowboy hat, were fixing a pair of stage lanterns to stands at either side of this unpromising performance space. It gradually dawned on me that they were two of the band's members. No roadies for these good old boys, then. No groupies. No sex and drugs. But, hopefully, a bit of rock and roll.

I mentally pictured Nick Simper and tried to make one of those faces fit. Neither did. At a table nearby, another couple of old boys who were clearly also in the band were sitting, chatting and swigging from Budweiser bottles. They didn't look familiar either. A doubt entered my head: was Nick Simper even going to be there? Had we chosen the one night on which he wouldn't be appearing? It was then that I noticed an open door close to the stage leading to— another room? Or outside? Perhaps he was out there somewhere. The guy in the cowboy hat went through this door in the kind of hurry that suggests some urgent business. Was it my imagination, but, as he left the clubroom, did I hear him say something like, 'Nick, have you got the…'

A moment or two later, he returned with another old guy.

'That's him,' I said.

'Who, Mark Simpter?' Karen asked.

'Who?'

'Thingy—'

'You mean Nick Si— '

'Oh, yes, Nick Simpter.'

'It's Nick Simper. Not Simpter. And yes, that's him.'

'Where?' Karen asked.

I nodded in the direction of the newcomer. He was not especially tall but was in good shape for his obvious age. He had grey hair that was long enough to cover his neck and he turned his head to reveal a slight bald patch.

'Are you sure?' Karen went on.

I nodded. Yes, I was sure. It was more than visual recognition. I felt a frisson pass through me as a dart that had been fired the second I picked up that copy of the Third Album in Lotus Records in the early eighties finally struck its target.

'Are you going to try to talk to him?' Karen asked.

'Yes,' I replied.

The truth, however, was that I was not as confident as I

sounded. I have always been conscious of my own shyness. As bullishly as I might talk about 'buttonholing' people, I've never found it an easy thing to do—particularly not to someone like Nick Simper who probably gets it all the time (although I had to admit that he was not exactly fighting the fans off at that precise moment).

Then there was the 'potential disappointment factor'. What if he turned out to be an egotistical prick? What if I went up to him and he turned around and told me to fuck off? He had always seemed like a nice guy in television interviews, but they were prepared; he was putting on a face. When caught off guard—well, who knew? Did I really want my illusions to be punctured in such a banal way?

For a few minutes, I continued to watch the band members busy themselves with their preparations. Then, an opportunity presented itself. Simper went to the stage and started to tune his bass guitar. He was completely alone. I was aware that I had gone to that club for a moment just like this one, but that wasn't what drove me. Instead, something inside me rose up and took control; I'm not sure what it was, but, again, I can only suppose that it was that long lost teenager in Stafford reasserting himself and demanding the chance for a little of the excitement, however vicarious, that his suburban world denied him.

'I'm going to go and talk to him,' I said, not waiting for a reply or really wanting one, but standing and, like someone in a trance, walking over to the stage.

Simper was facing away from me and bent over a guitar tuning gizmo. Great, I thought, I finally meet a former member of Deep Purple and I'm staring at his arse.

'Excuse me,' I said and, not being heard, again, more loudly, 'Excuse me!'

Simper half-turned.

'Yes?'

'Nick Simper?' I asked.

'Yes,' the reply came back.

'Hey!' I said, 'I am a huge fan of Mark I Deep Purple and would love to get a picture—of me with you, I mean. Would that be okay?'

'I'm tuning up,' he said, not really turning towards me.

Shit, I thought, this is not going well. He sees me as an irritant.

'Give me a minute,' he added.

That sounded more promising.

I stood there for a few moments, looking, I have little doubt, like a self-conscious fool while Simper twiddled with machine heads and monitored dials. He finished and stowed away his instrument. As he did this, I burbled:

'I'm a huge fan of Mark I. Do you ever listen to those albums?'

'Not really,' he said.

'I love your bits—like the bass line to "Chasing Shadows".'

'I've been doing some of that stuff in Austria,' he told me.

'Yes, with Nasty Habits,' I said, 'I've got your CD of that.'

He seemed impressed with this. It was just obscure enough to prove that I was a genuine fan—plus, it happened to be true: I did indeed own a copy of The Mark I Deep Purple Songbook CD by Nick Simper and Nasty Habits.

'We're doing a DVD,' he said, 'Filmed a concert—it's coming out soon. You won't hear any of that stuff with The Good Old Boys.'

'Bit more straight rock and roll?'

'We do "Hush" at the end—without a keyboard. Not quite right, but we give it a go. It gets a bit loud by that stage.'

'I'm looking forward to that!' I said, 'Could I get that photo?'

He stepped over to join me. I took out my iPhone and pointed its reverse camera towards us both. He put his arm around my shoulder.

'Is that how you do this these days?' he asked.

I laughed and nodded. One press of the camera image on the screen and a picture of me next to Nick Simper (my picture showing me with what looked like an enormous double chin) came into the world.

But my meeting with my hero was not over. He was a nice guy, after all, and was happy to stand around chatting for a bit.

'This isn't the usual sort of place we're asked to play,' he said.

'You were invited here?'

'Yes. But it gets bit loud. Looking at the audience—'They might need to turn down their hearing aids?'

'We might need to change things around a bit.'

'I saw you doing the Fleetwood Mac song "Oh Well" on your MySpace page.'

'Well, we're very loud by then! So, are you a member here?'

I told him 'no' and that I had come just for the gig from Cambridgeshire via Nottingham, adding: 'You're one of my icons! I've listened to a lot of your stuff—Warhorse, too.'

'Pete Parks, our guitarist, the guy with the long grey hair, was in Warhorse.'

'And, as I say, I do like Mark I Deep Purple.'

'Well, we do "Hush". You know, I listened to the original Billy Joe Royal version of that and it didn't sound much like our version—surprisingly different. But we just started playing it, adding different instruments and we ended up with what we had.'

I could hardly believe this! I was standing there listening to Nick Simper describe to me the origin of one of the great songs of my life—and saying things that I had not read in any interview!

'It's considered by everyone to be a Deep Purple song,' I said.

'Well,' he said, 'The Kula Shaker version is a remake of Deep Purple's take.'

'Yes,' I said, 'and the sound of the song has been really influential—The Charlatans' whole act is more-or-less based on it.'

He looked a little non-plussed.

'I don't really know about that stuff,' he said, 'I'm not really into it.'

I could sense that the conversation was over. There was no

point in broaching the subject of Rod Evans; I could think of no plausible way to bring it in and I would gain nothing by annoying someone who was so central to the story I wanted to tell. So I shook him by the hand and said how great it was to meet him. I returned to where Karen was sitting.

'I can hardly believe that you just went over there!' she said, 'I was really amazed!'

'He's just a guy,' I said with an insouciance that belied the nerves I had felt throughout the whole escapade.

'Did you ask about—'

I cut her off with a shake of the head.

The room began to fill up. It was a truly eclectic mix of people. A toddler with a dummy in his mouth ran around in the spaces between tables. A trio of very old people sat at the table next to us. Groups of teenagers and young adults drifted in and distributed themselves around the room. An older couple asked if the chairs at our table were free and, on learning that they were, sat opposite us. She was one of those women who age well enough for it to be difficult to judge how old she is—beyond being able to make some general statement to the effect that she must have been at least in later middle age. He was tall and slim, his small quantity of remaining hair grey and close cropped. He wore glasses and looked like nothing so much as an accountant having a night off; I was to be proved surprisingly—pleasantly surprisingly—wrong on that one.

The house lights went down at just after nine o'clock and those two lanterns picked out the stage. The show was about to begin!

A few twiddles on the guitar got things off to a low-key start before the band launched into a tight, entertaining run through of Clapton's 'Crossroads'. 'Hound Dog' was next. The shape of the gig was beginning to emerge. As singer Alan Barratt—he was the one in the cowboy hat—said during one of the breaks between songs, the set list had little to do with the various groups that the

Boys had once been in, being just a collection of the songs they liked—almost all covers—and enjoyed playing. Rock and roll standards dominated, with the likes of 'C'mon Everybody', 'Shakin' All Over' and 'Twenty Flight Rock' getting hugely enjoyable airings. There were also a couple of instrumentals, 'Sleepwalk' and a lovely version of The Shadows' 'Apache'. A little funk did creep in on a track called 'Shaky Ground'.

But the two highlights for me were numbers that did have their origin in some of the band members' erstwhile careers; the first was Hudson-Ford's 'Pick Up The Pieces' sung by Richard Hudson himself (who served as The Good Old Boys' drummer) and, of course, that version of 'Hush' that Simper had talked me through earlier on.

A few couples from the audience were sufficiently moved by the band's efforts to get up and jive; or, rather, they jigged about doing that girl-under-the-man's-arm thing that is the only jive step anyone actually knows.

Throughout the gig Barratt's banter centred largely around his age and that of his band mates. He played the amnesiac old codger, claiming at various points to have forgotten when he first encountered particular songs or who originally sang them. Although the chat was kept to a minimum, there was some nostalgia in what was said—perhaps even a smidgeon of wistfulness, as when Hudson's past as a member of The Strawbs was revealed. When the band introductions were done late in the set, the 'boys' were presented in ascending order of age. Nick Simper was described as 'the oldest and wealthiest'. When they played, though, these old men demonstrated beyond all reasonable doubt that age has got nothing to do with someone's capacity to rock; they really were five good old boys belting out the tunes and having a great time.

Midway through the set, there was an interval of about twenty minutes. The couple at our table asked if we could keep their seats and moved off. Idly, I watched them move around the room. My assumption had been that they were members of the club and were off to catch up with a few of their friends. To my surprise, they made a beeline for different members of the band with whom they seemed to be well-acquainted and in whose presence they were comfortable and at ease.

I was puzzled.

Did the quiet couple from across the table know the band members personally? If so, how? In my imagination, I began to construct scenarios in which these two were fellow Deep Purple aficionados, perhaps even Good Old Boys groupies who followed the band around, popping up at gigs around the country. The only problem with this theory was that they did not approach Nick Simper....

They returned to their seats just before the resumption of the gig. I decided to put my mind at rest.

'Are you members here?' I asked.

'No,' the woman replied.

'We're friends,' the man added, 'Of the band.'

'How do you know them?' I pressed.

'I was in a band in the late sixties that was part of the same scene,' the man said.

'Really?' I said, amazed.

'Yes,' he went on, 'I knew some of them—Jon Lord and so on—before they formed Deep Purple.'

For the second time that evening, I was struck by a revelation. A man who was of direct relevance to my quest sitting, by complete accident, directly opposite me!

'He was in The Flowerpot Men, wasn't he?' I glossed, 'And The Artwoods.'

'That's right,' the man confirmed, 'The Artwoods. I knew him then. We were all part of the same scene.'

'What was your band called?' I asked.

He did tell me, but it sounded like a complicated sixties name and was lost in the considerable amount of ambient sound.

'What did you play?' I asked.

'The guitar,' he said, 'It was funny. We all used to think that Jon Lord was ancient—he was so much older than the rest of us. He was twenty seven!'

It was strange how much that evening was turning into a disguised symposium on the passing of time. As happy in their own skins as The Good Old Boys seemed to be, they must have longed for those far-off days, just as the man I'd mistaken for an accountant clung so tenaciously to his one tentative connection with what they represented.

The Strawbs, Renaissance—these were big names once and you can go to a record shop practically anywhere in the world and pick up a CD with Nick Simper's picture on the cover. The forty three years that had passed since the release of Deep Purple Mark I's third, and final, album had been ones of—well, what?—for Nick Simper...dreams chased.

Disappointments.

Fleeting moments when fame promised to return...perhaps regrets, too—a sense of business unfinished, the loss of colleagues and, in Jon Lord, whom he had known before Deep Purple, the loss of a friend (he has spoken of this in TV interviews). As much as Alan Barratt joked about time, there was more poignancy to his words than he may have realised.

The man sitting opposite me, the guitarist, he knew. And how much more so would a certain other person embody the melancholy sentiment if he had been there?

And that certain other person? Well, who else?

Rod Evans, of course.

5—One More Rainy Day

IT WAS KAREN who suggested that we try to get the Good Old Boys to do a private gig, so I got on to MySpace and wrote the following email:

> *Hi!*
> *I saw your show at the social club in Nuneaton—outstanding! You've gained two fans! So much so that I wonder if you do private engagements? Various members of my family—including myself—have some quite big birthdays coming up and it would be amazing to celebrate with a Good Old Boys gig! Don't worry—I'm not talking about you strumming away in the corner of my lounge! Mind you, I am not a big corporation either, so there is a strict budget and, for that reason, this is very much a preliminary enquiry. I would, though, be keen to find out if you are available and, if so, what your fee would be.*
> > *Cheers!*

I clicked 'send' and sat back, playing the waiting game. My hope was that I would get more response than my message on Nick Simper's homepage had elicited.

Amazingly, a reply came back from one Lindsay, who ran the Boys' MySpace page. The mail said that, yes, the band did do private gigs and that, if I provided a phone number, Richard

Hudson himself would be in touch to arrange a booking. Richard Hudson of The Strawbs and Hudson-Ford! I sent back my details in a near febrile state of anticipation.

By interesting co-incidence, Richard called me while I was driving to a conference at Loz's school—and a meeting with Loz himself. I returned the call once I had checked into my clean and comfortable, but entirely conventional, hotel.

'Hello?' I said, 'Richard? It's Adrian.'

'Hi, Adrian,' the response came back.

The voice was mellow, aged, friendly. It was not the sardonic and arrogant drawl of some TV-smashing rock yob, but the warm tone of a favourite uncle.

'I was told that you might be prepared to take a private booking,' I said.

'Yes,' he came back, 'When were you looking at?'

My head was spinning a bit. I mentioned a time near to my birthday, some six months in the future. We agreed on a date and a fee (which was hefty, but, given the careers these guys had had, not excessive) and pencilled in my booking. I told him I would get back to him with a venue, which was 'likely to be in the West Midlands'. He was happy with that. The conversation came to an end.

I felt happy, exhilarated. Me a rock promoter—of sorts. There was another irony, of course: I had spent thirty years listening to Deep Purple and now there I was making an arrangement to employ one of them.

The next day was spent attending talks and round-table discussions with policy-makers and 'opinion-formers' on education. Loz came out to my hotel in the evening for a few drinks and to chew the fat. I had a couple of glasses of sauvignon blanc while he, since he was driving, stuck to Diet Cokes. I told him about the forthcoming gig; he listened in wide-eyed amazement as I reported the process by which I had secured the services of the Boys.

We talked about our shared love of classic rock—or Jurassic rock as it has been unkindly called. I was surprised to hear that Loz was not just what Karen had described—with a characteristically elastic approach to the English language—as a 'Deep Purpler', but was a big fan of the band Yes. I told him that I, too, had listened to a fair bit of their output and had even attended a gig in 2004 at the NEC that had seen the most highly regarded Yes line-up, including Jon Anderson, Steve Howe and Rick Wakeman, wheel out some of their greatest hits for a rare live airing.

'I really like 'Going for the One',' I said, 'That's on the album Tormato, isn't it?'

Loz put me right: 'No, it's on Going for the One—it's the title track.'

Yes, there was an album called Going for the One, now he mentioned it; that had slipped my mind. 'What's on Tormato, then?' I asked.

We racked our brains; nothing sprang immediately into either of them.

' 'Wondrous Stories'?' I tentatively suggested.

'That's a great track!' Loz opined.

I told him that it was one of the ones the band had done at the NEC gig.

They had also done 'Owner of a Lonely Heart' from the later 'comeback' album 90125 (or '90210' as Loz and I misremembered it) as part of an acoustic mini-set in the middle of the show.

'You know,' I said, ' 'Owner of a Lonely Heart' was the first track I ever heard on CD.'

He looked curious.

The broader context to the story is that CDs had appeared as a fabulous new music format way back in 1982 amid a blaze of press coverage and publicity. Their big selling points were that tracks could be accessed at the touch of a button and that the discs themselves were virtually indestructible. I remember seeing a news item on the BBC's now long-defunct magazine show 'Breakfast Time' in which a reporter had smothered a disc in honey before wiping it clean, placing it in a player and looking impressed as it belted out, with ne'er a crackle, 'Stayin' Alive' by the Bee Gees. Of course, this robustness proved to be something of a chimera and, once CDs became more mass market, manufacturers' advice was to treat them with the same care that generations had lavished on their vinyl albums.

Anyway, by the time I reached university, in 1986, the format had yet to make much progress and was still regarded as somewhat niche, if not elitist. One of the first people I met at college, however, was a guy called Chris, a second year undergraduate, who seemed to possess everything he wanted, including that most precious of objects, a hi-fi with a CD player plugged into it. He actually lived in a bedsit in the Summertown district of Oxford and, one night, a group of us went out there to drink and do whatever else students at the time did.

Chris's bedsit was like most such places: insular, gloomy and permeated with a musty smell of unwashed dishes, half-eaten take away cartons and skid-marked underpants. Chris himself was a larger-than-life character who, in one year at Oxford, had already earned himself a certain amount of notoriety in the main student newspaper and around the Union Society.

He was large framed, usually unshaven and a chain smoker. He talked incessantly about sex, almost always in the context of how pitifully small was the number of us who were actually getting any. His contempt for virgins (a word he spat out like a mouthful of curdled milk) was palpable; given that not only myself, but almost everyone else present, was, at that time, largely untouched by female hand, it was difficult not to feel at least mildly rebuked by his attitude. Nevertheless, there was something oddly glamorous—indeed, dazzling—about Chris: he seemed to know everyone worth knowing (even if he didn't get on with all of them very well) and he was the first very intelligent person I had ever met who liberally peppered his speech with swear words.

He was also cripplingly insecure and it was inevitable that, at some point, he would use his material possessions as a way of boosting his self-esteem. The hi-fi served this purpose admirably. Switching it on (with the remote control—I'd never seen that done before) elicited a flicker of wakefulness from its LED graphic equalizer—a gizmo that sounded impressive even if it served no discernible function.

'What shall we listen to?' Chris asked.

There was a pile of CDs near to where I sat and, dumbly, I picked up whatever was on the top and handed it over. It was 90125. Another press of a remote button made the CD drawer slide out obediently. Chris loaded the CD and hit 'play'. Almost immediately, the Trevor Horn-produced (or, over-produced) sound of 'Owner of a Lonely Heart' smashed its way out of the vibrating speakers. Of course, with its power chords, multiple layers and brassy synth inserts, the track could have been specifically engineered to demonstrate what the newish format could do, but it was no less a revelation for that.

I was blown away.

This was a million miles away from the tinny, flat sounds of the various record and cassette players I had thitherto been used to; this was music with a third dimension to it. Thanks to Yes (and Chris), obtaining a CD player and a collection of the magical little shiny discs that fitted into it became my obsession du jour. Strange to think that even the technological marvel that was CDs is now old hat and on the verge of checking into Hotel Oblivion for a rendezvous with its old mate, vinyl.

In a different, very real, hotel, Loz sipped his Diet Coke as he pondered this anecdote.

'The thing is,' he said, 'that they were—are—excellent musicians. Those old rockers, I mean. They didn't really need CD technology to make them sound good. Look at Deep Purple. They're best live. Brilliant. So much better than pop stars today.'

'Mark I, too,' I offered.

'Absolutely!'

'Those first three albums were very experimental,' I went on.

'But,' he said, 'when you listen to In Rock, it sounds amazing. Even now. I mean, it is just incredible; could have been recorded yesterday. I know that Mark II's first release was 'The Concerto'— 'Which is very under-rated.'

'It's bloody good! Particularly the vocal section. That's just beautiful.'

'It must have been composed before Gillan joined, though,' I said, 'I wonder what Rod Evans would have done with it?'

'Concerto for Group and Orchestra', as we have seen, was indeed Deep Purple Mark II's first official release but, in many ways, it is a Mark I product. It was written, on the hoof, by Jon Lord while the Rod Evans-fronted line-up was touring and, musically, it has more in common with the first three albums than the hard and heavy sound with which the band would shortly make their name.

Like much of Mark I's output, there is a very large element of experimentation about it, the stated aim being to end the cold war between classical and popular music by bringing the two together in a composition that would allow each to showcase what it does best while complementing and, occasionally, contrasting with, the other. Divided into three movements, all of the members of the band get their own solo moments, while the orchestra is given the chance to shine with music that roves over a variety of tones and textures. It must be said that the whole thing is surprisingly entertaining—even if for many it is more than a little baffling.

Listening to it now—as I find myself doing with unexpected frequency—I'm not sure whether it qualifies as a work of genius or a hubristic folie de grandeur. For a little known—at the time— combo like Deep Purple to book the Royal Albert Hall and engage the services of no less an orchestra than the Royal Philharmonic conducted by Sir Malcolm Arnold was, by any reckoning, an audacious move. That there was huge potential for something to go wrong was underlined by Ian Hansford, who spoke of how he and Mick Angus sat in the front row praying that Ian Paice would get through the concert without damaging a drum, there being no way of stopping the show to bring on a replacement.

Vocals are confined to the second movement and feature Ian Gillan in one of his best performances, one that surely earned him the gig to essay the title role on the first ever recording of Jesus Christ Superstar a year later.

Famously, Gillan is supposed to have written the Concerto's lyrics on a napkin the day before the performance. That he was against the enterprise is well-known and is betrayed in what he sings, which is surprisingly mean-spirited at times; he is certainly not coy about his feelings in such lines as:

> *What shall I do when they stand smiling at me?*
> *Look at the floor and be, oh, so cool*
> *Oh, so cool?*
> *How shall I know when to start singing my song?*
> *What shall I do if they all go wrong?'*

That said, there is some genuine poetry in the first couple of verses—to the extent that it is difficult to accept the claim that Gillan had given no thought whatsoever to the lyrics until almost the last minute.

These days, though, clicking on the 'play' icon of iTunes does bring to mind the question I posed to Loz in that hotel bar, namely, what would Rod Evans have made of it? After all, Evans would have been the singer that Lord had in mind when he started the Herculean labour of writing the music.

Whatever might be said of the lyrics as they stand, it must be conceded that Gillan found a rather lovely melody to sing them to: would Evans have managed the same feat? It is tempting to think that he might have done as good a job, but the evidence suggests otherwise. It is all too easy to believe that he would have come up with another banal love narrative and a clunky melody that would have served in a workmanlike way, but not put too great a burden on the memory. The counterpoint between the lilting beauty of the melody and the acerbic lyrics in the version that we have at least challenges the listener; few Rod Evans songs are particularly challenging.

I put this speculation to Loz. He agreed. Neither of us could really see a Rod Evans centred Concerto being anything other than a disaster. We sat quietly for a while, pondering on what we had said, two old rockers with power chords going around in our heads.

As I sipped my drink, I could not help wondering what makes someone invest so much love in a band? I would say that it's reminiscent of the devotion people can have to a football club (or, perhaps, any other sports team), but I am not entirely sure that that would be correct. Following a football team is a tribal thing, often not really offered as a choice. For example, my team is Birmingham City, 'the Blues'. I support them not because they are successful— 'Blues glory supporter' is a contradiction in terms—or even because they represent my hometown—I have never lived in Birmingham.

No, I support them because my father did—and his father did before him. It's a family tradition, one that's caused me a great deal of misery over the years, all of which I could have avoided if I had gone my own way and made my own choices. But I didn't and the Blues are now so ingrained in my DNA that it would be unthinkable to abandon them.

I have, however, often wondered what, exactly, it is that I support. It is not the specific individuals who make up the team: they change all the time and the men who ran out on to the pitch when I saw my first game back in 1974 are now of pensionable age and not what you would call match fit. It is also not any meaningful connection to the area in which the club is located. The players are not, on the whole, from Birmingham; in many cases, they are not even English. They are thus not representing their local community. Many of them, quite frankly, are not even Birmingham City fans themselves.

So what do I support?

I think it is an idea. The idea of Birmingham City embodied in a badge and a set of colours. It does not matter who plays for the club or what their motives are, because the club is greater than them all—greater than us all. Greater than me.

My love for Deep Purple is not like that. Yes, it's true that the composition of the band's personnel has been unusually unstable, but that has not really been equivalent to the constant merry-go-round of players at a football club. The different versions of the band have had distinct identities and many fans attach themselves to particular 'marks' while decrying others (Mark I suffers more than its fair share in this regard).

As a fan, you therefore feel a relationship to the individual members of the band; unlike with a football team, it is a personal thing. You feel that the band members are, in some way, your friends, talking directly to you. This can, it must be said, lead to a certain loss of perspective at times: I regret to say that even I have invested words of frown-inducing triteness with undeserved gravity because they have appeared in an interview with one of my Deep Purple heroes.

But, then, that's what being a hardcore fan is all about. And I am not, as it happens, just a hardcore music fan. Comics are also a big thing for me. Especially science fiction comics—although I am not completely impartial to a little superhero action and am proud to own original runs of a short-lived monthly called 'Marvel Superheroes', a flimsy British 'Hulk Comic' and—the icing on the cake—a full, pristine set of Alan Moore's 'V For Vendetta'. I must say, though, that my favourite has always been '2000AD', which has changed many times over the years, but has always featured the rather bloodthirsty adventures of Judge Dredd.

I say 'always', but interestingly, Dredd's first outing in the comic was in issue two, the very first edition's hopes resting largely on a revival of that icon of stiff upperlipness, Dan Dare—and I should know because I was one of the thousands who bought it.

The year was 1977 and my Deep Purple obsession lay in the future. In fact, at that point, I owned no music at all and, to be honest, showed little interest in it, even for one of such tender years. Comics were my world; so much so that my parents frequently expressed their dismay at my lack of any other reading. My first foray into the world of comics had been with an utterly inane 'humour' title called 'Monster Fun', which featured such mirth-free tales as 'Creature Teacher', 'Terror TV', 'Gums (a shark worse than its bite)' and, its one concession to the serious, 'March of the Mighty Ones' in which Britain is evacuated after some robot dinosaurs escape from somewhere (don't ask); apparently, only a couple of kids have the wherewithal to stop these mechanical rotters.

By the ripe old age of nine, I was growing out of such nonsense and so I moved on to a notorious British title 'Action' which was principally characterised by its breathtakingly graphic levels of violence. A story called 'Dredger' (which was about hard-bitten spies) showed someone being murdered by a dowsing of sulphuric acid. 'Hookjaw' meanwhile gleefully depicted scene after scene of people (often bikini-clad nymphets) getting their limbs and heads ripped off by hungry man-eating sharks, while 'Death Game 1999' had men who played 'spinball'—a futuristic sport with more than a passing resemblance to Rollerball—splattered against walls, run over by spike-tired motorbikes and generally brutalised in pursuit of a winning goal. The comic was not, however, without an educational side: from a story called 'The Running Man', I learned both how to bottle someone and how to convert a pocket full of loose change into an ad hoc knuckle duster.

'2000AD' was essentially 'Action' with a sci-fi twist and it was every bit as violent. The story 'Flesh' was typical; this explored the rather neat idea of people from a food-crisis-hit future travelling back in time to hunt dinosaurs and, inadvertently, become the cause of their extinction. Naturally, nothing much ran smoothly for our protagonists and each installment was full of carefully-drawn extras getting eaten by dinosaurs or crushed by dinosaurs or accidentally mixed up in the meat production process and thus ending up as an unlisted ingredient of dino-burgers or saurian sausages. Characters that we had followed for weeks were cynically and unceremoniously dispatched, heroes and villains were virtually indistinguishable from each other and the whole thing came to a weird and horrific conclusion in the present day.

Every issue of '2000AD' featured a body count that made the Battle of Stalingrad look like a picnic. One service that the comic did do, though, was to be the place that first introduced me to a little film that was coming out called 'Star Wars'. I remember it distinctly: the first ever '2000AD Summer Special' included an article on the film laced with some extremely intriguing pictures of Darth Vader and a group of Imperial Stormtroopers.

'Star Wars' became another obsession for me at that point.

To make the connection with Deep Purple, it can be said that the film had a decidedly rock 'n' roll sensibility to it: it did not have the same rhythms as other films made at the time. It was fast-moving and frenetically cut together. Later interviews with the editor suggested that this was often because director George Lucas had not filmed enough material and so rapid cuts had to be made before the ends of scenes in order to disguise the fact. If this is so, then it was a happy accident, because it gave to the film a pace and drive that were as much a part of its success as its lauded special effects. I remember going to the cinema with my sisters and mother a couple of weeks before 'Star Wars' opened (to watch 'The Spaceman and King Arthur' or some such long-forgotten kids' movie) and seeing a trailer for it. My mother was genuinely delighted by what she saw and leaned over to me to whisper, 'It looks really exciting, doesn't it?'

'Star Wars' was not part of my childhood; it was my childhood. For this reason, George Lucas's constant tampering with it has, to me, the lustre of Stalin airbrushing his opponents out of old photographs.

Sci-Fi, superheroes, 'Star Wars'. My childhood, yes. Then I grew up a bit and heavy rock, and, pre-eminently, Deep Purple, became my adolescence.

So there's the answer to my original question. Or, anyway, an answer.

What makes someone invest so much love in a band? The same thing that makes them invest time, interest and—we might as well say it—love in a comic or a film or whatever: these things are part of yourself. They make you who you are. Perhaps that's why it's different from supporting a football team. Become a football supporter and you surrender to the greater entity that is the team and its followers. But love a band, love a film, love a comic and you are defining your individuality. It is the type of love that makes you who you are; the love that makes you special.

Loz and I finished our drinks. We said our farewells and he headed off back to his school. I went up to my room, thinking about rock bands and comics and the fans who keep them going. I had rarely felt happier to be a hardcore fan than at that moment.

I was to come crashing back down to earth only a matter of weeks later.

It was a 'nothing special' sort of day and I had been wondering where to hold the Good Old Boys gig and generally pottering around. I had looked at the websites of a few clubhouses in the West Midlands and, as you do, I happened to access Facebook. During my wanderings around that annoyingly addictive corner of the Internet, I had signed up to receive updates from the official Deep Purple website, most of which consisted of video clips of old interviews and occasional bits of live footage.

On July 16th 2012, I logged in to be presented with one of the most depressing status updates that I can remember. There in front of me was a picture of Jon Lord and beneath it, these few words:

We are all deeply saddened by the news that Jon Lord has passed away today at the age of 71 after suffering a pulmonary embolism. He had been suffering from pancreatic cancer and was surrounded by his family at the London Clinic. Our most heartfelt sympathies go to his family. Jon Lord, a giant among men.

I was stunned. I read it again. Could it be true? Jon Lord gone? Something profound shifted in my world. I remember when Elvis Presley died in that fateful year, 1977, my mother had commented that it was like a part of her youth ending once and for all. As a child I had found that statement a bit strange, but now it made perfect sense. A part of my childhood, my young adulthood—hell, my older adulthood!—had died.

As the Facebook post said, it was known that Lord had been ill. An announcement had appeared some months earlier on the Deep Purple Appreciation Society homepage that he was suffering from an unspecified cancer, but was confident that he would get through it and be back at work sooner rather than later. An interview with Ian Paice that I caught on the Internet a short while later filled in more details, confirming that Lord had been diagnosed with pancreatic cancer (which Paice described as 'not a good one'), but that it had been caught early and, if anything, was going to cause less of a delay to the maestro's work schedule than had originally been feared. It seemed that the old dog had some life in him yet...

And then, one rainy July day, he died.

My first instinct was to text Loz. All I could think of to put was 'Jon Lord has died'. A response came back, 'That is very sad'. Perhaps it is the limitations of the medium, but that struck me as coolly detached. A short while later, a more considered, more moving text came through: 'It's such a sad day. He was one of my heroes. What an Englishman. What a gentleman. What a talent'. I could not have put it better myself.

Over the next couple of days, various media tributes to Lord appeared, including those from other members of the band. In a radio interview, Gillan recounted a story about how an excited fan had rushed up to Lord in an airport and, muddling his words, proclaimed, 'I'm your hero,' receiving the insouciant reply, 'So you're King Arthur.' Steve Morse put a highly personal and touchingly humble tribute on his web page and even the normally reticent Ritchie Blackmore issued a statement describing Lord as a great musician and his 'favourite dinner companion'. The Deep Purple fansite The Highway Star removed all of its content and simply displayed a picture of Jon with the label 'RIP'. One person who did not come forward to make his feelings known was Rod Evans, despite this being an excellent opportunity to end his self-imposed exile.

The key themes that appeared over and over again in the tributes were ones that Loz had inadvertently latched on to in his second, longer text: that Lord had been an outstanding musician, a true gentleman and that, in some way, he represented a, possibly anachronistic, species of Englishness.

Obituaries consistently described Lord as the man who founded Deep Purple, which was, in a way, true. Certainly, it was he who had been there at the start with Chris Curtis and it was he who had kept the vision alive as Curtis's increasing eccentricities threatened to scupper the whole project. There was also an emphasis on how much Lord had contributed to Deep Purple's sound, some rather hyperbolically suggesting that all of the songs had been built around his keyboard playing. As much as the general outpourings of grief can account for such claims, the fact remains that Deep Purple were always—as Lord was first to acknowledge—a guitar-led band, his contribution being very much in a supporting role. But—and here's the rub—it was a crucial supporting role. It was, after all, the keyboards that made Deep Purple different from other bands and it was the keyboards that provided the little symphonic and baroque touches that added a hint of elegance to songs that otherwise might have been nothing more than straightforward rock and roll run-throughs.

Most commentators highlighted the 'Concerto for Group and

Orchestra' as Lord's signature composition. For me, this was how it should have been and, in years to come, I suspect that the piece will be seen as not only his greatest work, but perhaps the most important release by the band. Lord had been working on a studio version of the Concerto—oddly, the first ever—until a couple of months before his death. On the various message boards that were attached to fansites and band member homepages, it was the Concerto that was mentioned again and again, along with other pieces in a similar vein. 'The Gemini Suite', Lord's second full-length attempt to integrate Deep Purple into an orchestral sound, was lauded as was, surprisingly, 'April', which looked set to win a re-appraisal as a lost Deep Purple classic.

If Lord's music elicited the bulk of the comments, his character also came in for much analysis and praise. Roger Glover's homepage included a statement that largely focused on this area, but Loz's text seemed to be repeated by someone or other wherever I looked. How much of a gentleman Jon had been was mentioned everywhere. Even to those of us who never met him, it was obvious that he deserved that overused soubriquet more than most. He was well spoken and polite—even to Hugh Hefner—and was always prepared to be the public face of Purple in interviews and documentaries. Perhaps, at times, he was a little too gentlemanly, lacking the edge to take on Blackmore at his own game and thus making himself complicit in some rather Machiavellian manoeuvres, such as those that saw the sacking of Rod Evans and Nick Simper.

Yet, this may have been as much down to the other facet of his character that Loz had so astutely identified, Lord's Englishness. Lord never pretended to be American as Glenn Hughes had done during the 1970s to the detriment of several Mark III and Mark IV live albums. His voice always had a certain East Midlands flatness behind the well-enunciated, perfectly grammatical, sentences it articulated. There was a reserve there, too. Lord was well known for always having time for his fans, regardless of how gruelling a just-completed gig might have been. This was, to be sure, a version of that vague, but rather English, quality 'niceness', but it was also a fear of giving offence, which, as any English person will tell you, can cause as much harm as good.

As for Lord's music, much of it has a distinctive Englishness to it. One of his late orchestral compositions is a piece called 'Durham Concerto' which was commissioned by that picturesque northern town's University. It is exactly what its title suggests that it would be, a celebration of the city in music.

Perhaps, though, it is that idiosyncratic Deep Purple mini-epic 'April' that is most distinctively English. After all, as a month, April is more significant in England than in many other parts of the world. It is traditionally a month of Spring rains, the time when the countryside wakes from its Winter slumber, when the temperature begins to rise, when, according to Chaucer, people long to go on pilgrimages and, for some reason, it is the start of the English tax year (which may explain why the Third Album's liner notes describe it as a 'sad month'). Listen again to the music: what goes through your mind as you take in the first section of the song? To me it's always the English countryside and the rather wan sunlight that characterises the English Spring and people on bicycles in little rural lanes and daffodils and blossoms...to me, the music is incomprehensible unless it is taken as the soundtrack to a vision of England.

I was listening to 'April' as I considered these things. Farewell, Jon. Godspeed.

But it all made my quest that bit more urgent. It was a reminder in the most upsetting way possible that the people I was dealing with were old men; they would not last forever.

Good Old Boys indeed.

6—Hush

SEVERAL POTENTIAL COURSES of action lay open to me. One was to contact every hospital in the San Francisco area and ask them if they had, or had ever had, a Rod Evans working for them. Even if this had been possible, I doubted whether an answer would have been forthcoming.

The second option was one suggested by Karen: to discover whether any of Evans' family were still around and to attempt to get some idea of his current location from them. This was promising, although a cursory search on the Internet implied that such information would not be easy to come by. The third was to keep on looking for Mick Angus.

My MySpace missive to Nobody's Darlings had elicited no response at all, which was hardly surprising since, according to the site, it had not been read. I got back in touch with the exotic-sounding woman from Thames Talent and asked her if she knew anything. Her reply?

> *Seems like Thames have never heard of the guy. Sorry that*
> *you're running into a dead end here.*

One possibility presented itself. In the mid-sixties, Evans had sung with a band called The Horizons, which had featured among its personnel Len 'Chip' Hawkes who had later gone on to play with The Tremeloes. The Horizons had morphed into MI5 and then The

Maze, the band from which both Evans and Ian Paice had migrated to Deep Purple. The connection was thus tenuous, but Hawkes was still active and, according to the Internet, relatively easy to contact. I hoped that he might know where the other ex-members of The Maze were hiding and, through them, there was a chance that I could construct a path leading to Mick Angus or, cutting out the middleman, Evans himself.

I logged on to Hawkes' homepage and was happy to see a dialogue box that would allow me to send him an email. There was just one problem: Hawkes was battling a fairly serious disease and, although all the usual noises about getting back to work soon were being made, I was conscious that much the same had been said of Jon Lord and that sending an email on a relatively frivolous subject at a time like that could well be viewed as rather tasteless. I ummed and ahhed a fair bit before persuading myself to go ahead with it because Hawkes was advertising some tour dates and I supposed that he would not be doing that if he was not responding well to treatment. I was also coward enough to hide behind the relative anonymity of email: at worst, I told myself, I would be viewed as an unwelcome nuisance and ignored.

I was ignored.

If those approaches were coming to nothing, it must be admitted that even my attempt to construct some context to the Mark I story was not as simple as I might have hoped it would be.

Take my planned trip to Highleigh Manor, for instance. You would think that such a grand-sounding place might be quite a prominent feature of the English countryside. You would be wrong. The Internet has apparently never heard of it. Putting the name into Google returns nothing more than a few property searches in the West Sussex area. There is also a map which—you would have to admit, usefully—gives the location of nearby postboxes. But there is no mention of a Manor.

I was interested in it because it was the place in which Deep Purple rehearsed the songs for 'Shades' before going into the studio. I had thought of paying the place a visit, but who can visit somewhere that doesn't exist? Besides, the chosen day was, climatically speaking, distinctly English in quality (i.e., wet, miserable and cold). The expedition to nowhere, then, was put on hold (i.e., abandoned).

Well, I thought, I can always go to the place where the recordings actually took place. This had been Pye Studios at ATV House in London's Great Cumberland Place. I didn't expect to find a fully functioning recording studio—or to be allowed into it even if I did—but it would have been enlightening to see what current use was being made of the building.

The answer was none. ATV House was no longer there, having been demolished some years earlier.

The ever-dependable Internet gave me some clues as to what it had been like, however. Old photographs showed a huge wooden mixing desk, reel-to-reel tape recorders, dials and indicators on which needles flickered against numbers to show—what?—volume, bass, treble? It was a reminder of those clumsy, but strangely exciting, pre-digital days.

According to a brief history of the studio that someone had posted on the web, a good number of well-known bands had recorded albums there, including The Kinks, MC5 and The Who. More enticing, though, were some of whom I had never heard, but who sported the kinds of names that had the sixties and seventies written all over them and who created some truly weird-sounding music. 'Owlcreek Incident' by Prelude was intriguing, but best of all was 'Afreaka' by Demon Fuzz. As I have said before, we no longer live in an age in which it is necessary to use one's imagination when confronted with the novel and unfamiliar; a quick scout of YouTube brought this particular bunch of psychedelic funksters to life in front of me. They were quite good, I thought. I was also delighted to see that Pye Studios had once played host to the Good Old Boys source band, The Strawbs.

What had the recording sessions for 'Shades' been like? I knew that they had been quick, as was the wont for sixties bands cutting their first discs. They had probably also been relatively ego-free. A flavour of what they may have been like can be gleaned from that footage of the band recording 'Wring That Neck' on which Rod Evans looks like he is sleeping.

Again, to imagine myself back into that scene was to be confronted with the deadening nature of time. As the tape rolled on Day 1, as the first chord was struck, the first cymbal sounded, the first key pressed, did any of those present wonder where it might lead? Would they believe, if it were possible to tell them, that they were taking the first tentative steps on a road that some of them would still be walking nearly fifty years later? Would Rod Evans have accepted that he would turn into a riddle wrapped in a mystery inside an enigma? Those old pictures were mute on that subject.

One happier outcome of this stage of my search was the discovery—at last!—of Mick Angus. My attempts to find him in America had proven futile because it turned out that he had, in fact, been living on the south coast of England for several years in happy retirement. It was Ian Hansford who made the vital connection, supplying me with a precious telephone number and the promise that Mick was willing to talk.

I called one Sunday evening. It was another fascinating conversation. For example, Mick told me a little more about the story of his audition for the role of Deep Purple vocalist. The version hinted at by Simon Robinson had only been partly the truth; according to Mick, he had responded to a 'vocalist wanted' advertisement in Melody Maker and, following an audition, had actually been installed as Deep Purple's lead singer. His fatal mistake had been to recommend Ian Paice as drummer for the fledgling band and it was to his audition that Rod Evans tagged along and tried out, only to be given the job over Angus.

This must have been especially galling for Angus, since, as he told me, he had known Evans since childhood. They had long harboured ambitions of rock and roll fame and, as youngsters, had made recordings of themselves singing in the type of voice-o-graph booths that used to be popular at fairgrounds and seaside resorts.

Angus had ended up as a Deep Purple roadie after starting a company with some former members of The Maze (it owned a recording studio that went under the intriguing title of 'Virgin Sounds'); while working at this, he received a letter from Jon Lord in America inviting him to get involved with Deep Purple; Angus told me that the choice between twiddling buttons and pushing faders in Windsor or joining the party with a rock band in America was not really a choice and he booked his flight as soon as he could.

As close as his relationship with Evans had been, Angus told me that he had not actually seen him since he left Deep Purple in 1969. Angus himself remained with the band until just before the Fireball album in 1971, after which, he had worked as a tour manager for such groups as the Bee Gees and as an executive for Capitol Records.

He recounted an anecdote about being at a nightclub in LA in around 1973 at which someone asked if he had seen Rod Evans, who was in the vicinity, but Evans, true to form, had already left the building before Angus arrived. The last time that Angus spoke to Evans was by telephone sometime around 1988 or 1989. I wondered why a friendship that had been so long-standing (lifelong, indeed) had been allowed to die so easily, but, from what Angus said, it had more to do with busy lives heading along diverging paths than anything sinister.

Mick Angus was certainly an interesting guy. My search for him had not been in vain because he could be the subject of a book in his own right, but, as a lead in the quest for Rod Evans, he was cold, a dead end. I was no nearer to reaching my goal than I had been before.

Still, the Good Old Boys gig was coming together. I had a venue booked and even an excuse for it—my Mum's seventieth birthday. In that respect, I felt that I was making some progress. In others, not so much.

It was while I was doing all of this that I began to conceive of the quest in slightly different terms. Initially, I had been intoxicated with the notion of finding Rod Evans and saw myself as some sort of hero to the fan community, unveiling the long lost singer to a grateful world. My optimism had been high as it seemed to me that the main reason for no-one having found him yet was that no-one had looked hard enough.

I realised that such an attitude had been somewhat naïve. Evans quite probably did not want to be found. Perhaps, then, I had no right to find him. But to understand this, we need again to step back into our time capsule of the imagination and head back to an earlier epoch.

It was 1980. Deep Purple were back! Or, rather, they weren't. Instead, a fake version of the band appeared and started to tour around parts of the USA and Mexico. A clip of this lot performing 'Smoke on the Water' is available on YouTube. Watching it is a painful experience. To call the standard of the musicianship poor would be to flatter it. The guitarist does not seem to know any of the song apart from the famous main riff which he just plays all the way through in a constantly repeating pattern. He also has no real clue about soloing, so the keyboardist fills in, adding some half-hearted organ licks that are so low in the mix as to be barely audible.

The drummer seems to be not only playing a different song, but playing it at an entirely different gig. At various points, the musicians act as though they do not know what is supposed to happen next, leading to some shockingly awkward segues between verses, choruses, instrumental sections and—well, who cares? They certainly don't. The whole thing is an embarrassment. And not just any embarrassment; this is a gouge-out-your-eyes-as-punishment-for-making-you-look-at-this-stuff embarrassment.

But, in the middle of this debacle, one guy stands out, soldiering bravely on, his slightly stocky frame accentuated by a figure-hugging white t-shirt as he bawls into his microphone while gesticulating animatedly with his free hand: it's the lead singer. He battles gamely against both the hideous cacophony going on around him and the blatant hostility of the crowd. He even seems to know some of the lyrics. The strange thing is, though, that the voice is vaguely familiar. Yes, I'm sure I've heard it before and, now I think about it, I'm sure I've seen the guy himself somewhere or other.

It's Rod Evans.

His presence is what turns the clip from high farce to tragedy. It is a record of the last time that Evans performed in public; indeed, as far as I am aware, it is the last time he was seen on any kind of public platform. The clip is cringe-inducing for certain, but, beneath that, it is sad, a testimony to folly and the cynical exploitation of folly.

The story can be told quickly and simply. While living in America, Evans was approached by an unscrupulous manager who proposed to make him the centrepiece of a reformed Deep Purple.

Nick Simper was also sounded out, but wisely turned down the offer. According to Ian Hansford, it was Evans himself who had made the approach, but Simper was out when the phone rang and, when his wife passed on the message, he expressed no wish to return the call. Evans, however, was more easily duped and agreed not only to the misguided enterprise but to becoming its sole shareholder, meaning that he bore full financial—and legal—responsibility for whatever might transpire. Four non-entities (who, on the strength of that YouTube clip, were barely musicians) were recruited to be the other members of the band and a tour was booked.

A number of shambolic, and, if reports are to be believed, brief, gigs, were played in the USA and Mexico, the set lists of which included Mark II and Mark III songs to which Evans had no connection. That did not, allegedly, prevent him from introducing one, 'Might Just Take Your Life', as being from 'our Burn album'.

Although the 'genuine' band had split up some years earlier, their business affairs were still being looked after by a management team and it was only a matter of time before their ire was invoked.

They stepped in with the double whammy of a court injunction and a newspaper advert warning potential ticket buyers that what they were being sold was a fraud. Legal action followed, resulting in a huge damages award, for which Rod Evans was personally—and exclusively—liable. It was the end for his share of royalties from the Deep Purple albums on which he featured and the end for any hope of a continuation of his musical career since any earnings from such work would merely have gone to paying off the damages.

So many questions and issues follow from this sorry tale that it is difficult to know where to start.

It might be asked, for example, what Evans actually did wrong in the legal sense (leaving aside the wrong his 'Deep Purple' did to the music). As an original member of the band, his claim to its name was pretty strong and, after all, if his version of the band only included one original member, then much the same can be said of the 'official' Deep Purple that continued to tour after Jon Lord's retirement in 2002.

The main mystery, however, is just what it was that made Evans get involved with what many sources have described as 'some very bad people'. A fool could have seen that he was being used by dubious operators out to make a fast buck from a brand name with which he was associated. Was that his motivation, too? Or was the whole thing conceived as a form of revenge on his erstwhile Purple colleagues, people against whom he might have held an understandable grudge?

Reading interviews he did at the time, it would appear not. He told the music weekly Sounds that he was keen to get back into rock and roll having lost interest in the medical career that he had pursued after his departure from Captain Beyond. He described his commitment as long-term and talked about releasing multiple albums with this band, going as far as to say that he could see the music heading off in a more progressive rock orientated direction than had been the case with Deep Purple's previous offerings.

He seems, then, to have viewed this new Deep Purple as a serious comeback with a potentially bright future. To be fair, he may not have been entirely without good reason to. That the band was offered a contract by Warner Curb Records, a subsidiary of the same Warner Bros Records that issued 'genuine' Deep Purple's product in the United States (a link that, obviously, no-one at the parent company spotted) is a matter of fact. More than this, songs for a putative album were written and recorded. Only two of these are known about: 'Blood Blister' and the Spooneristically (and provisionally?) titled 'Brum Doogie'.

No tapes of these are thought to exist and you will search Google in vain for the lyrics or sheet music of either. The band's guitarist, Tony Flynn (who, it must be said, is a far more accomplished musician than that 'Smoke on the Water' clip would suggest) has put live performances of a few songs on YouTube, at least one of which—'All I Am is Blue'—may have been originally intended for the album, but this is hard to verify and cannot be stated with much certainty; if it was, it is more enjoyable than might be expected, although not very 'Deep Purple' in style.

Flynn is not the only musician associated with this fake version of Deep Purple who is still active. The rest of the band is still knocking around, too, and I even managed to get hold of someone who knows all of them. He told me that they are all very resistant to talking about what happened in 1980. Certainly, a Facebook message that I sent to Dick Juergens, the drummer, did not receive any kind of acknowledgement. One can sympathise. The musicians may not have been as personally exposed as Rod Evans, but their reputations were not exactly enhanced by their roles in the sad little escapade.

What can be said of it all is that Evans was apparently blind to the glaring truth that his idealism was not shared by many, if any, of his collaborators. The Sounds interviewer asked, perfectly reasonably, why he chose to perform numbers from versions of the band that came after his involvement had ended, rather than focus on Mark I material (according to one source with whom I spoke, the 1980 Deep Purple did include some Mark I songs such as 'Hush' and 'Mandrake Root' in their set). There is no need to go into the answer Evans gave, but, in essence, it was a fudged admission that no-one would have wanted to hear that. It was further put to him that he could have realised the ambition to get back to what he loved doing by starting a new band and promoting it as being led by the original singer with Deep Purple. More fudging, more justifying the unjustifiable.

Of course, he could have done as the Sounds interviewer suggested. That is what every other ex-member of Deep Purple was doing at the time. He would not, perhaps, have had the same impact as Ritchie Blackmore had with Rainbow, or David Coverdale had with Whitesnake, but the Mark III bass player, Glenn Hughes, has had a successful, albeit low key, solo career spanning nearly forty years. He even managed a late highlight when his band Black Country Communion hit the (mildly) big time in 2010, 2011 and 2017.

Evans could well have followed this example, concentrating on material that suited his voice and building a grassroots following, spiced up with the odd interview or talk about Deep Purple and some lucrative dates playing with a tribute band. He could have done that. But he chose to take a huge gamble based on incomplete information. It was a gamble he lost.

And so he disappeared. He lost all contact with the rock world in which he had played a small, but significant, role and the many fans whose enthusiasm and love keep it turning. In the wake of the court judgement against him, he became a recluse, or, more likely, he went into ordinary life, carrying a damages bill that he could never hope to pay off, together with, it can be imagined, a heart full of bitterness.

Before this whole episode is moved on from, it is worth

recording a few thoughts about the attitude of the members and management of genuine Deep Purple. They do not come out of it well. There is something mean-spirited and vengeful in their actions that no amount of after-the-fact rationalisation can conceal.

In the Sounds interview, Evans implies that, if he didn't exactly get the blessing of Jon Lord and Ian Paice to go ahead with his new Deep Purple, they were rather indifferent to it on the basis that genuine Deep Purple was not, at that time, a going concern.

That certainly does not come through in the wholly punitive nature of the damages they sought. Was it really necessary to impose a financial penalty that many would see as wildly disproportionate to the offence caused? Paice's justification was that the band members never saw any of the money, as it all went on paying the costs of the lawyers who represented them.

Mmm...

Lord resorted to quoting Shakespeare in an attempt to argue that his chief concern was with his reputation, which was under threat from Evans' antics.

He may have had a point, but it is difficult to see how an outrageous damages award equates to greater restoration of lost face. For balance, it should be mentioned that genuine Deep Purple's lawyers did send a few 'cease and desist' letters before resorting to court action. How necessary any of it was is open to question.

The fact is, within a gig or two of Evans and his merry men hitting the road, there were few illusions among either the public or the press about what was going on. Whether intentionally or not, official Deep Purple destroyed Evans' career and, probably, bankrupted him, without gaining anything of substance apart from a return to the status quo ante.

That was it, then. The last anyone saw of Rod Evans—as far as anyone knew, anyway.

So where did that leave my quest?

I began to feel that, perhaps, finding the man himself was less interesting than exploring his world—and mine. After all, that is pretty much all I had managed so far, but the process had not been unrewarding.

So, as of now, this becomes the story of me trying to piece together a portrait of Rod Evans from circumstantial evidence, but also of discovering more about those old rockers, what they did and where they are now. It's also about myself and all the other fans, those who generate the love on which the whole creaky, leaky boat keeps sailing.

And—who knew—perhaps I would still come up with some way to find Rod Evans himself?

7—I'm So Glad

THE WEEK LEADING up to the Good Old Boys gig was weird in all kinds of ways. For a start, a new Pope was being elected in Rome. Beyond the fact that much of my family consists of Irish Catholics, this had little to do with me.

Of more immediate concern was the weather, which was unseasonably cold—to say the least. This was—in case I haven't mentioned it—the middle of March and the UK was gripped by blizzards. Actual why-does-a-little-bit-of-snow-bring-the-country-to-its-knees style blizzards. I was anxious about the possible impact on audience attendance. More worryingly, the nightmare scenario of the Good Old Boys cancelling had high odds of coming true: these were not young men, remember.

The gig was to be held in Stafford, where my narrative began all those pages and decades ago. The venue was a sports club, chosen because I knew from experience that the Boys could rock such a place. I had arranged to take—along with Karen—my friend Tosh.

Half-Indian, half-Scouser, Tosh was blighted by partial sight, but blessed with an excellent ear. Perhaps as a result, he had a phenomenal knowledge of music. It was a rare band or singer that was not represented somewhere in his collection; in fact, it was a rare album that he did not seem to own. Some of his tastes were ones of which I wholly approved; he was, for instance, a huge Rolling Stones fan and could identify the source album for any named track. He could—indeed, would—give the year of its release, too (a habit I quickly began to find annoying). Some of his pronouncements on music were, however, ones with which I had rather less sympathy. His insistence that Karen Carpenter was the greatest female vocalist of all time seemed a bit left field to me and his almost idolatrous love of Jethro Tull was one that, in spite of my best efforts, I just could not share.

The plan was simple. I would pick up Tosh from his flat, drive us up to Nottingham in my two-seat—and, therefore, reasonably useless—roadster. We would then meet Karen, grab some lunch, transfer into her bigger, more practical, car and head over to Stafford for the gig. We would all be staying that night in my Mother's pied-a-terre flat in Lichfield. What could possibly go wrong?

Over lunch in a trendy wine bar in Nottingham (sample menu item: Halloumi stack with celeriac remoulade and fries), we talked through the possible answers to that one. My chief concern, the weather notwithstanding, was that the band would not turn up. My only real contact with them had been the exchange of a few emails with Richard Hudson. I had offered a deposit, but that had been politely declined, meaning that there was no guarantee that they would be there as arranged.

My worries were exacerbated by the fact that I had already cancelled on them once, having moved my original proposed date back by three months when I was hit with a bout of chronic inability to get myself organized. I would not have blamed Richard if he had seen me as some sort of delusional joker who was not particularly serious about the whole thing. The hastily-conceived Plan B was to buy a blue tooth speaker and play some music from my iPhone—if, of course, the worst did indeed happen. To say that this might have disappointed the audience was something of an understatement, even if the audience did consist only of guests at my mother's birthday party.

In order to reassure myself, I had emailed Richard Hudson a

few days ahead of time just to make sure that he and the others still intended to come.

Forty eight whole hours had passed before a reply came back telling me that—yes!—the band were all looking forward to the gig. Richard also informed me that he would be playing the previous night with a different band in the decidedly un-rock 'n' roll town of Market Harborough which was not too far away and from which he would have easy access to Stafford. Despite this apparent confirmation of the booking, my mind was not really put at rest; somehow, I just could not quite believe that people such as Nick Simper and Richard himself were actually going to be playing for me!

The next snag hit once we arrived in Stafford. I had used the internet to plan a route to the venue. Upon reaching journey's end as indicated by the printed-out directions and map, nothing that could even charitably be described as a sports club was visible. We drove around for nearly half an hour trying to find something before, belatedly, I decided to check the address on the venue's website. I immediately realised that I had programmed in the wrong postcode—which created the next problem: what if I had sent the wrong postcode to the band? Pointless conversations between the three of us in the car led to the resolve to simply go to the correct venue and hope for the best.

The club proved to be more-or-less what might have been expected: a pleasant function room with a bar and a food serving hatch. It had a low ceiling, a few tables with chairs around them and a large plasma screen TV that was, at that moment, showing the England Rugby team's humiliation at the hands of Wales for the benefit of four or five increasingly disgruntled men who I took to be members. On the hopeful side, a drum kit had been set up in the corner of the room: that had to be a good sign.

It was because of the drum kit that I had a better look around and noticed the other guy in there, sitting on his own, patiently watching the game. He was on the short side, slightly built and as bald as myself. I wondered if…but, no…that would almost be too much to…but, remembering the Nuneaton gig, I did have to say that he did look a bit like…

I decided to make absolutely sure. One of the club's two barmaids was buttering some sandwiches—I assumed for the party—in the small kitchen area and I approached her, making up some question to do with whether she knew anything about the band's current whereabouts. She pointed to the bald guy: 'He's something to do with it.'

I had been right. I approached him. 'Richard?' I asked.

'Yes.'

The guy stood up.

'I'm Adrian,' I said.

He had a thin and kind-looking, but well-weathered, face. It was a face that told—or could have told—a lot of stories. He seemed grateful that someone connected to the booking had finally turned up. I was struck by the irony. Clearly, he had suffered exactly the same worries as myself about whether the event was actually going to take place. But, finally, we had made a connection and there was a palpable sense of relief in the air. Relief and a new-found purposefulness: we could both now get on with doing what we needed to do secure in the knowledge that no-one was going to let anyone down.

There was one issue, though: where was the rest of the band?

'They'll be here,' Richard assured me.

Given that they would mostly be coming up from London, I had to wonder, but, given that there was nothing I could do about it, I put the matter to the back of my mind.

'Have you been here for long?' I asked.

'Since about three.'

It was now just after six.

'You've been here for three hours?'

'Yes. I stayed with a friend in Market Harborough but he was going out today, so I thought I would just head over and get set up.'

It was not until I was halfway through my first beer that I was struck by the thought that someone with a major international rock career in his biography had just spent three hours sitting around watching Rugby on the television while waiting to play a gig in celebration of my mother's birthday.

On the one hand, that gave me an odd sense of importance, but, on the other, it brought home the banality of the life that professional musicians lead. Even famous or once-famous professional musicians—yes, there are moments of glory, but most of it is just earning a living, taking jobs where you can and playing to whatever crowd you can cobble together. On a darker note, I also began to feel weirdly exposed with doubts beginning to creep in: would this evening live up to the band? Would the audience be large enough for them? Would it be the right sort of audience? Had I, in fact, done nothing more than bring them all the way up from London under false pretences?

My fears were in no way assuaged when my mother and stepfather joined us a little later and I introduced Richard to them. True to form, my mother started to gabble on to him about the catering and how much food there was and how there would be lots to spare and that a doggie bag would probably be needed and...

Richard took it all in with a gracious smile and a degree of indulgence that totally belied the image of rock stars as arrogant and egotistical. Nevertheless, I was forced to take my mother aside and lay out some ground rules:

'Can you do me a favour,' I said, 'and not bore the shit out of rock legends?'

She agreed.

As we waited for the rest of the band to arrive, I sat at one of the tables with Richard and we passed the time in idle talk. I swigged on my beer (for the record, he did not take up my offer of one, claiming that he only liked to have a drink after about seven o'clock: I suspected that this was something of a change from how things had been 'back in the day'...). I asked him about the

Strawbs. He told me that they had had some success in America and had toured there extensively. He also told me about how he now spent a lot of his time running a company that handled the band's royalties, having won back the rights to their songs from whichever publishing company had originally taken them—together with a handsome cut, I imagined. From what he was saying, he still enjoyed a steady income from his back catalogue and who could begrudge him that? But, it did remind me of how those contemporaries of his, Rod Evans and Nick Simper had lost their slices of the royalty pie for Deep Purple Mark I's output.

If I were to sum up Richard in one word, it would be 'modest'. He downplayed his achievements, demurring to the Strawbs' singer, Dave Cousins, as the band's main creative force ('He had to sing the songs, after all; they needed to fit his voice') and refusing to see what he did as anything more than a job that just happened to involve the thing he most enjoyed. The conversation meandered around the music that he played and that I loved. He asked me about the bands that I had seen live and I told him about Deep Purple and Yes and some of the others. He told me about his other project, The Beaky Band, which I was delighted to hear was a collaboration with the very same Beaky from that most eccentrically-named of sixties pop groups, Dave Dee, Dozy, Beaky, Mick and Titch. It was the Strawbs, though, to which we kept returning.

I was reasonably familiar with their output, but, having got into The Good Old Boys, I had gone back to it and listened to as much of it as I could find on Spotify and YouTube. While it is undoubtedly rock, quite what adjective should go with that word is difficult to ascertain. There is more than a hint of the bar room about their biggest hit 'Part of the Union' (co-written by Richard), but 'The Battle' is a lengthy baroque fantasy with narrative lyrics set to music that follows the sweep of the story from quiet opening to violent centre to poignant end.

'Thirty Days' touches on the psychedelic in its use of a sitar and 'Lay Down' is a catchy, driving anthem. Song titles like 'The Flower and the Young Man' and 'Witchwood' are perhaps the best signposts to the Strawbs' sensibilities: if the band was anything, it was folky, but, then, perhaps, it would be simpler to say that it wasn't 'anything' in this sense.

Perhaps the point was that it was not easy to pigeonhole, that it was just a collection of musicians expressing themselves with an extra-ordinarily wide range of instruments that led to the songs being unusually heterogeneous in style. They were creative, dramatic, experimental, atmospheric, but not any one thing and, as a result, never boring. Were the band 'art rockers', then? I doubt that they would have said so.

What they undoubtedly were, or had been, was big. In his book, The People's Songs: The Story of Modern Britain in 50 Records, Stuart Maconie puts 'Part of the Union' on his list of hit singles that could be called era-defining, or, at least, era-embodying. Indeed, with its wry take on industrial relations, it can be viewed as the unofficial anthem of the mid-seventies malaise, the days of strikes, economic stagnation and power cuts. It is, though, a distinctively British take on events, conjuring up a speaker who clings tenaciously to the modicum of power that he gets from being 'part of the union', but without ever patronising him; as a song, it is both even-handed and affectionately humorous.

My conversation with Richard was interrupted by the ringtone of his mobile phone.

'That's the singer,' he said, checking it, 'Which is good because he's bringing the PA.'

He got up to take the call. I rejoined Tosh, Karen and my family members, who had all ensconced themselves in a corner to catch up on recent developments in their lives.

'How's it going, mate?' Tosh asked.

'Well,' I replied, adding a little more ruefully, 'I just hope the rest of the band get here. He's taking a call from the singer, so I suppose he will make it.'

'You could have them play drum and vocal only versions of the songs.'

'That is an option,' I replied, somewhat distractedly.

By now, Richard had completed his call.

'Is he coming?' I enquired.

'He's here! He's outside.'

Relief again swept through me like a reinvigorating wave. It seemed that some sort of critical mass had been reached; if these two had made it, then surely the others would, too.

The singer, Alan Barratt, came in through a rear 'stage door' into the venue. He was shorter than I remembered and wore a loose-fitting shirt, jeans and the battered old cowboy hat he had sported in Nuneaton. If anything, his face was even more of a mini-novel than Richard's, but it was every bit as kindly, his most common expression being one of laid-back tolerance, punctuated with occasional easy smiles. The two of them began to set up, bringing in amps, mixing boards and cables from outside and using them to assemble a stage area in and around the drum kit.

Meanwhile, the party was beginning to pick up steam. The buffet arrived. Mum had not been wrong: there really was enough food to make the Feeding of the Five Thousand look like a hastily-grabbed snack. Guests started to appear. There were, it is true, a few younger people there—cousins, grandchildren and the like—but the majority were older, Mum's age or thereabouts. Hence my next source of worry: would the gig be too loud for them? The space was not, after all, particularly big, and the ceiling, as I have said, was low.

The potential for the place to rapidly turn into an unbearable cauldron of sound was quite high. There was also a dance floor, a small dance floor, admittedly, but, insofar as I could see little prospect of it actually being used, it might as well have been the pitch at Wembley Stadium, a vast, pristine emptiness stretching out in front of me, taunting me with the reality of a failed dream.

I was so busy hearing from various old people about how they had not seen me since I was 'yay high' that the first I realised that the rest of the band had arrived was when the twangs, crunches and thrums of tuning up began to emanate from the area around Richard's drum kit. Strangely, I felt almost blasé about the fact that Nick Simper was now in the room and no more than a few metres away from where I stood. The time that I had spent talking to Richard had had the effect of bringing it all down to earth, of turning these musical icons into ordinary guys for me and even, dare I say it, almost-friends.

And, on an equally positive note, there was a good number of guests. The room was filling up and I was more and more confident that I would be providing the Boys with a worthwhile audience. It was with feelings of slightly edgy anticipation that I tucked into a plate of sandwiches and small pastry things as, ahead of the gig, the buffet was dispensed with. Karen gave my arm an encouraging squeeze while Tosh divided his time between eating, quaffing beer and smoking outside.

The lights went down, the audience sat or stood expectantly. Without ceremony, the band launched into their opening number, 'Hound Dog'. To my delight, the dance floor was almost immediately populated with enthusiastic jivers. That was when I knew that all of my fears had been misplaced. It was going to be all right. It was going to work. I relaxed, allowed myself to smile and went with the music. Song followed song, followed instrumental number, followed song.

'What do you think?' I asked Tosh as he stood contemplating a foray on to the dance floor.

'Awesome!' was his apt review.

The gig was turning into a triumph.

Admittedly, a few guests left early on the grounds that the music was too loud for them (one couple cited the bizarre reason that it risked bringing on one of the wife's migraines), but most stayed.

As the evening wore on, I found myself enjoying

conversational cameos that gave me a feel for just who comprised the audience I had assembled. I learned, for example, about how, in the fifties and sixties, a guy from Florida who was there with the band, had played guitar in various outfits with Nick Simper. He proved to be a man of strong views, regaling me with his take on American politics. Barack Obama, he said, was a 'moron' and a 'fucking idiot' who did not 'know what he was doing'. I felt it best not to argue.

Then there was the husband of one of my Mum's friends who informed me that the band's music was exactly what he liked and that anything from later than the 1950s was 'crap'. He went as far as to say that, 'even the Beatles' were too modern for his taste. I also enjoyed my conversation with a grey haired, rather cadaverous-looking old woman who reminisced about her days as a 'massive fan' of Deep Purple and, indeed, such Deep Purple spin-off bands as Whitesnake and Gillan. As much as I found this hard to picture, I had to remind myself that, when those bands were starting up and, indeed, at their peak of success, she would have been relatively young.

Two of my aunts added a little extra colour, too. One, who I had always thought of as rather straight-laced, belied my long held misconception by remaining firmly on the dance floor all evening energetically jiving, before gushing at length about how much she loved the band. The other spent the period before the start of the gig attached to Richard Hudson and Alan Barratt, hanging on their every word like a geriatric groupie.

During the interval, Tosh, outside on one of his frequent fag breaks, bumped into Nick Simper, who was getting a bit of fresh air. Quite what they talked about, I cannot say, but Tosh told me that he found Simper to be a 'humble man' and not at all the ego-driven self-obsessive he might have been. In this respect, Tosh was touching on a common theme from my dealings with these former stars.

The rock continued to roll once the gig recommenced and,

eventually, the last few songs approached. Alan began a verbal introduction to 'Hush'. He said:

> *Things have changed a bit since the good old days. We're getting on a bit. Mind you, we're all still on drugs. Oh, yes! Statins. Blood pressure tablets. Heart pills. All sorts of drugs.*

Given the average age of the audience, this one went down well. Behind him, the familiar bouncing bass line of Deep Purple's biggest hit started up.

'This is one for all of you,' he said.

Then they were into it. The whole evening seemed to be summed up by that song. I am not sure what my feelings were. Obviously, it was an invigorating and consummately entertaining part of the show. But, for me, the thought that it was being played by one of the men who had recorded the original single, the original hit single, the single that had taken America by storm, that had made Deep Purple In Rock and 'Smoke on the Water' possible, that was a bona fide piece of rock history—and it was being played here, in this unprepossessing little room in Stafford to this private audience of my family and friends—it was an emotional moment.

The last clang of the guitar reverberated to nothing, the bass gave up its dark throbbing, the final thump of the drum was a decisive full stop. The gig was over. The audience was left delighted and thrilled by what they had seen and heard. I stepped over a cable into that magic zone occupied by the band. Richard sat behind his drum kit, hot, but smiling.

'What can I say?' I said, 'That was amazing! Thank you so much!'

'Thank you!' he replied, 'Look at the band; they've loved this!'

I surveyed the faces of the musicians. He was right. In the words of Jon Lord, you could have spanned the Thames with their smiles.

Later, Karen, Tosh and I, having decamped to my Mum's flat, sipped nightcaps as we reflected on the evening.

'That was awesome!' Tosh repeated.

To be fair, he was doing no more than give voice to the thoughts we all were having.

'You didn't get to talk to Nick Simpter, did you?' Karen said.

'It's Simper,' I said, 'and no, I didn't really.'

'You could have asked him about Rod thingy,' she said.

I could have done, but, as I told her, Simper had repeatedly denied any knowledge of Rod Evans' whereabouts. Besides, I could not really bring myself to see it as particularly important at that moment. The temporary tinnitus of those post-gig hours was still reminding me of the experience I had just had, the music, the people, the sheer joy of it all!

More than that, it was telling me that I was alive and life was good! The quest could wait.

This was a moment to savour.

8—Wring That Neck

A COMMON PROBLEM faced by the Deep Purple hardcore fan—indeed, by most fans of hard rock music—is that one's partner/s is/are not very likely to share his (and it is usually 'his') tastes. I have certainly found this to be the case throughout my life.

While my ex-wife was supportive enough to attend a couple of Purple gigs with me, the music was never really her thing. Her preference was for the lighter, the poppier, the mellower. Her favourite bands were eighties wine bar mainstays Everything But The Girl and David Bowie. Neither of these is a bad choice, you understand, taken on its own terms. EBTG were excellent musicians who happened upon a pretty unique style of jazz-infused pop. For me, though, they were a little too slick, a little too glib, a little too 'lounge'.

Bowie, it need hardly be said, is widely acknowledged as a musical genius and I would say that I like him, too, except that the inevitable follow-up question would be, yes, but which Bowie do you like? It seems to me that his musical experiments are so diverse that it would be nigh on impossible to pinpoint exactly what constitutes the 'Bowie sound'. Is it the whimsical balladeering of 'Space Oddity'? The heavy rocking of 'Jean Genie'? Or the camp cabaret artistry of 'Boys Keep Swinging'?

As for live acts that we saw together, those two DP gigs notwithstanding, it was an eclectic mix. There was the night, for example, that we went along to Birmingham's Symphony Hall to hear The Penguin Café Orchestra. One of my ex-wife's favourites (much to the bemusement of more conventional friends of ours who could see little merit or entertainment value in their music) the group was an avant garde ensemble that made use of a wide variety of instruments and sound effects in the creation of their, admittedly distinctive, tunes. They were open to a plethora of influences, mixing Celtic folk with world music beats and repetitive, hypnotic rhythms. At their best, they produced work of mesmerising beauty; at their worst, they were just a little boring.

Another time, we again went to Symphony Hall to catch a live outing for saxophonist Jan Garbarek and his then-collaborators the Hilliard Ensemble. An unlikely combination of free form improvised jazz and Gregorian Chant, the music works well enough on record; in a live context, it simply did not come off. What is haunting, lilting, even relaxing, when played as ambient music from a CD, became a gruelling 90 minutes of monotony and incongruity.

So much for my ex-wife. Other partners also had different ideas from me when it came to music. A couple of girlfriends who were themselves highly accomplished musicians listened primarily to classical pieces, helping, along the way, to develop my tastes in that area. Yet another was essentially a pop fan, filling her house with chart sounds and easy listening tracks.

Karen's natural inclinations music-wise are rather broad. Although her list would be topped by world music, dance tunes and the folkier end of pop, she is willing to give anything a listen. The two of us have spent many a happy evening at concert venues and in jazz clubs while energetic hip hop groups have pounded out their rhythms or Django Reinhardt impersonators have picked away at their guitars. We have seen grand operas and listened to the harmonic gorgeousness of choral works.

On one memorable occasion, we found ourselves in a place called Jazz Land in Vienna, a venue that in no way belied its name by showcasing a fabulous collection of musicians who filled its cellar-like space with some wonderful extempore playing. Just as often, we have sat on my sofa with a glass of wine or a shot glass of whisky revelling in the genius of Miles Davis or John Coltrane. We do not—as you would probably expect—always agree and have had many a heated discussion about the validity of reggae as an art form. Speaking personally, I cannot stand it, finding it dull and rather self-important and I have done my due diligence on this, having been to more than one Caribbean Carnival with the intention of getting a bit more into the culture behind the music—to no avail.

More positively, some of Karen's attempts to share her tastes with me have worked out rather better. She got me along to a festival in Nottingham, for example. True, she was keen to see one band and I was more excited by others, but, at least we were there together and we did concur in heaping praise on the second-on-the-bill Blondie (for the record, the headliners were The Scissor Sisters, who, it has to be conceded, 'gave good gig'). We also went along to a festival in the Derbyshire countryside that gloried in the title of 'Bearded Theory', coming away with a newfound love of the Sheffield-based band Reverend and the Makers.

All of this is by way of bringing me around to one area on which we suffered no disagreement at all, The Good Old Boys and their various offshoots. Keeping my word to Richard Hudson, we went back to where our relationship with the band had begun—that sports club in Nuneaton. Our aim was to see the Beaky Band and, hopefully, to have a chat with Richard between sets.

Quite where the quest for Rod Evans was at that precise moment would be hard to say. If it was not actually dead, it was definitely more than a little moribund. Still, it had at least led me to that strangely significant venue in Nuneaton, which was beginning to look like an interesting enough outcome in itself.

A little research into the band we were about to see threw up the surprising fact that the eponymous 'Beaky' was not, in fact, the original owner of that name. I had assumed that 'Beaky' had been specific to a particular individual. Apparently, this was not the case, it being more a stage name or even a character that could be played by anyone—or, at least, anyone strumming rhythm guitar for Dave Dee, Dozy, Beaky, Mick and Tich. I discovered that the original Beaky, John Dymond, had left the band after a hiatus in Spain to be replaced by Paul Bennett. He, in turn, dropped out in the early 1990s, his place—and title to the name 'Beaky'—being taken over by Tony Carpenter. It was the last of the three that we were going to see.

We arrived after the gig had started, largely because our ability to navigate the outskirts of Nuneaton was in no way enhanced by our having done it before. Richard Hudson was ensconced behind his drum kit and thus more-or-less invisible from the floor. Centre stage was held by 'Beaky', an affable-looking guy in jeans and t-shirt with the standard-issue longish and straggly-ish hair of the aging rocker.

The band was tight and talented, but they did not make the same impact on me as The Good Old Boys had done. In part, this was down to the fact that, for all his charm, Beaky was just not an Alan Barratt. Barratt, one felt, was a rock and roller who did what he did and didn't give a fuck whether anyone was listening. Beaky, on the other hand, was too eager to please. It was not difficult to imagine him on the bill at a holiday camp alongside a superannuated stand-up comedian who had never made it and a hopeful ventriloquist who never would. He was not helped by a set list that lacked any real coherence or sense of direction. Light pop and soul numbers rubbed shoulders with old standards and harder-edged fare such as 'Born to be Wild' and ZZ Top's 'Tush'. I think that even a bit of Tom Jones' back catalogue slipped in there somewhere. I struggled to see what sort of appeal the band might have, or even be trying for.

That said, the assembled crowd was appreciative, enthusiastically applauding each number as it ended and playing along with Beaky's banter. Evidently, Beaky was a better judge of the audience than I was and a better judge of his audience in the wider sense of that word.

The interval came and Richard Hudson descended for a beer. I apprehended him at the bar.

'Richard! Hi! How are you?'

Gratifyingly, he recognised me straightaway. He offered me a beer; I declined and bought him one instead.

'How's your Mum?' he asked.

I told him that Mum was well and we exchanged a few pleasantries about her birthday party.

'I loved the gig,' I said.

'So did we,' he replied, repeating what he had said on the night.

'The band—' I meant the Good Old Boys, '—were really tight.'

'Well, that's nice to hear because you know they don't rehearse.'

I was amazed.

'What? Not at all?'

'I try to get them to, but they just make excuses.'

I was impressed: 'Well, if they can do that without rehearsing'.

'I've written a couple of songs for the band,' he went on, 'but they would need to be rehearsed and getting the guys together to do that is next-to-impossible. It is impossible.'

I was intrigued to hear this.

'Original songs? You've written original songs?'

'Yes. A couple of things. I thought that they would slot into the set list nicely. Hasn't happened.'

I am not sure whether the germ of an idea started to form at that point or whether it came later…as the second half of the gig got under way, I put it to Karen: 'What about trying to get The Good Old Boys together in a recording studio to lay down Richard's original songs?'

'What would you do with them?'

'What the band or the songs?'

'Well, both really.'

'The songs,' I said, 'could be uploaded to iTunes or put on to CDs to sell at the band's gigs—that wouldn't cost a lot.'

'It's worth looking into, isn't it?'

That it most definitely was. The only drawback, of course, was that I did not have a recording studio. I knew someone who I hoped could be prevailed upon to produce an EP, but where to do the recording? Were there any favours that I could call in?

9—April, Part 1

AS I PONDERED such matters, Deep Purple's story continued with the release of a new studio album, their first in nearly seven years. Far better than anyone had a right to expect, it enjoyed some glowing critical reviews and very respectable sales (it even briefly made it into the UK top 20, the first Deep Purple album to do so since the 1980s).

In the euphoria of a recent successful release, there was talk in some interviews of a follow-up coming along more quickly than had been the case of late.

I was sceptical of this.

The album's title, Now What?!, alludes to the passing of time and, indeed, this is very much a theme of the whole thing. The lyrics of one song begin, 'Time it does not matter / But time is all we have'. It is not all cod philosophising, however, the song 'All the Time in the World' being from the viewpoint of a character who has wasted his life but, vainly, tells himself that it is not too late to get up and do something useful or meaningful after all. 'Vincent Price' goes further in exploring the possibility of rising, vampire-like, from the grave! For all that, if the album was not quite a swan song, it was at least an admission that the night was closing in.

This impression is reinforced by the fact that Now What?! is the first piece of recorded material produced by the band in the wake of Jon Lord's death. The song, 'Above and Beyond', indeed, is explicitly a tribute to the great man. With lyrics such as, 'You touch me in the darkness / I send you a sign' and, most memorably, 'Souls having touched / Are forever entwined', it seems to be giving us the imagined words of Lord from the other side of the grave. It is also a means by which the members of the band expressed their grief; as such, it is a moving, as well as thrilling, piece of rock.

Another commemorative event was to be the following year's Sunflower Jam at the Royal Albert Hall, subtitled 'Celebrating Jon Lord'. The Sunflower Jam was basically a charity concert featuring various old rockers which had been held every year for a while and was becoming something of an institution. Of it Jon Lord had been a consistent and vocal supporter and to it he had been a frequent contributor. On this occasion, many of Lord's erstwhile friends and collaborators were to be present, with Deep Purple themselves topping the bill.

As soon as it was advertised, Loz got in touch suggesting that we attend. It was to be held on a Friday night, meaning that I would have to get from my place of work (which was not in London) to London in the early evening—and still trust to luck and the vagaries of public transport in order to make the start time. Logistically, it would be a challenge, but there was no way that I could resist the chance to see so many of my lifelong heroes together on a stage; I accepted Loz's invitation and decided to worry about how to make it all work later.

Thus, at five o'clock on an April evening I stood on a platform of Peterborough railway station mentally planning a journey that, God willing, would allow me to keep my agreed rendezvous with Loz. The weather was mild, but I had had no chance to change into appropriate clothes, putting me in the odd position of being about to attend a rock gig dressed in a jacket, shirt and smart shoes. Although I had shown some abandon in removing my tie, I was keenly aware that I would represent a stark contrast to most other audience members.

While waiting for the train, I wondered if the choice of month had been an accident. Whether or not it had any relevance to Deep Purple's back catalogue, it did seem—perhaps accidentally—appropriate to the King Arthur-loving man in whose memory the gig was being held.

T S Eliot, for one, describes April as a month in which rituals of death and resurrection were once held by primitive societies hoping to get Spring going by giving Nature a gentle nudge. To Eliot, such fertility cults are linked to the quest for the Holy Grail, the suggestion being that the discovery of that mystical, and somewhat ill-defined, object would bring to an end a winter-like state of inertia and sterility that could be either physical or, more probably, spiritual, and which might affect either an individual or an entire society. It would be a little hyperbolic to suggest that the Sunflower Jam was to be the equivalent of an ancient fertility rite, but, in a way, it was to do with resurrection. Jon Lord had passed away; nothing could alter that. But, his music remained and to play it was to bring him back, albeit temporarily.

I met Loz outside the Royal Albert Hall. He was the opposite of me, looking unshaven and casual, having been on holiday from work for the past week. He was also remarkably thin—the most obvious benefit of his training regime for the forthcoming London Marathon.

'How are you doing?' he asked as I approached him.

'Very well,' I replied as we shook hands.

'This is going to be cool!' he said.

I could only agree. The chief effect of the dash across London in which I had just engaged (apart from leading me to contemplate an application for a job as a live organ courier) had been to get my adrenaline pumping, which had, in turn, raised my excitement levels to rarely before seen heights.

Our tickets shown, we went in and began the lengthy climb up several flights of stairs to the balcony seats that, meanly, were all that we had been prepared to pay for.

I had been to the RAH before, of course—most memorably

for the revival of the 'Concerto for Group and Orchestra' in 1999—but it never fails to impress me. There is something TARDIS-like about the place. Yes, from the outside it looks big, very big even, but, compared to a modern arena, it's not especially overwhelming, a feeling enhanced by its setting opposite the expanse of Hyde Park.

Go inside, though, and you are presented with a space that can only be described as enormous. The auditorium is a perfect circle with the stage at one edge, a stalls area directly in front of that and balconies and gods stretching up ever-more vertiginously towards a domed ceiling that curves over all like a lid that can barely contain the sounds beneath it.

The audience was the same collection of the old and faithful that I had observed at the concert in 2011 when Deep Purple had toured with an orchestra. I had—not surprisingly—walked past a group of them on my way to the venue. They had all been middle aged and all wearing the de rigeur hard rock t-shirts. I had overheard one describing the history of the band to an equally middle aged wife or girlfriend who was clearly there under duress; sweetly, he had been in the process of recounting the tale of Rod Evans' departure as my late-for-a-meeting march overhauled their early-for-a-gig amble. It was one of those moments when I felt an odd sense of belonging: I was no different from such people, after all, and they are the real heroes and heroines of this story.

As Loz and I took our seats—gently balancing the plastic glasses of lager that we had brought from the bar—we speculated on what the set list might include. We knew it would be a mix of rock and classical, but the list of performers made guessing difficult. I was fairly certain that Deep Purple would include the Jon tribute song from 'Now What?!' (I was to be proved right about that) but had little clue about anything else, especially what the orchestral pieces would be. We both hoped for some representation of the 'Concerto' but that was as far as our surmises went.

We did not have to wait long for an answer. The show began

in low key style with the master of ceremonies, 'Whispering' Bob Harris—best known for presenting the 1970s rock television show, 'The Old Grey Whistle Test'—introducing Ian Paice with Jon Lord's widow, Vicky, who read an emotional message of gratitude to the fans for all of their support.

It was a nice moment that served to unite everyone in the room and create a tone for the first part of the evening, which focused on Lord's classical works. Sections from his composition 'Sarabande' were interspersed with a movement from 'The Durham Concerto' and a number of the songs that he had written in an attempt to fuse rock music with a classical backing and sensibility; the best received of these was 'Pictured Within' sung by Lord's long-time collaborator, Miller Anderson.

I enjoyed it all, although Loz was less impressed, describing it in diplomatic terms as 'tricky'.

Fortunately for him, post-interval, rock predominated. Paul Weller was an unlikely addition to the bill, but he ran through a couple of old Artwoods songs with considerable aplomb; two numbers from the back catalogue of the Purple-hiatus trio Paice, Ashton and Lord were aired by an ad hoc group, as was a lovely orchestra-backed duet of the Purple minor classic, 'Soldier of Fortune'. Mark III bassist Glenn Hughes earned a good deal of applause for his triptych of Purple tracks (with Iron Maiden vocalist Bruce Dickinson joining in on two of them) before Deep Purple came on to run through a few songs culminating in a long—and rather brilliant—jam-heavy version of 'Hush' on which everyone present took a role—everyone, that is, apart from Hughes, a no-show that neither Loz nor I failed to notice.

Loz and I were of one voice in seeing the star of the show as Ian Paice, the brilliant, too often unsung, and hugely modest, drummer who has appeared on every Deep Purple album—the only person who can make that claim.

As evenings go, it was undoubtedly memorable, but it was often memorable for reasons that I would not have predicted in advance. Jeremy Irons' reading of a Thomas Hardy poem over one of Lord's more delicate compositions, for instance, silenced the crowd. Paul Weller's contribution was a standout moment and even Glenn Hughes—not usually my favourite ex-Purple person—managed a powerful fan-pleasing performance. There was even a funny and heartfelt tribute from that old stager, and Lord family friend, Joe Brown.

Nevertheless, the event was as notable for its omissions as its inclusions. The dropping of 'Smoke on the Water' from Deep Purple's set was close to shocking, but proved to be surprisingly welcome, a reminder of how a world famous classic can be as much a burden to a group as a blessing. Less easy to explain, or forgive, was the total absence of anything from the 'Concerto for Group and Orchestra'. The second vocal movement would have gone down a storm and, since both Ian Gillan—its original singer—and Bruce Dickinson—who essayed the part on the studio recording—were present, it would have been eminently performable. To me, there was a resultant hollowness at the core of the evening, as though someone had published an edition of Shakespeare's complete works but had decided against including 'Hamlet'.

Even more startling were some of the gaps on the guest list, with neither Ritchie Blackmore nor David Coverdale choosing to involve themselves. In the case of the former, an allowance can perhaps be made; he had, after all, recorded a tribute to Lord (called 'Carry On...Jon') with his band Blackmore's Night and had made it known that that was to be his way of memorialising his late friend and colleague. Fair enough, but it is harder to accept Coverdale's non-attendance.

Had Coverdale turned up, the possibilities for some once-in-a-lifetime reunions abounded. The presence of Hughes and Paice, for example, made a Deep Purple Mark III get-together eminently feasible (this combination plus Blackmore is almost too much to dream of...). Moreover, the version of Coverdale's band Whitesnake that is remembered with most affection featured not only Lord, but Paice, Bernie Marsden, Mickey Moody and Neil Murray—all of whom were there. In both instances, Coverdale was the missing link.

For my purposes, the most marked black holes in the bill's constellation of stars were those too often neglected figures from the Mark I days, Nick Simper and Rod Evans.

Quite why Simper did not appear is anyone's guess; perhaps the organisers simply forgot to invite him. He would have had a far greater claim to be there than a sizable proportion of the artists who did turn up and he would have been more familiar to the Deep Purple fans who comprised the bulk of the audience.

As for Evans: if I had fantasised that, at some point in the show, an old man with grey hair, a weathered face and forgiveness in his heart would stand behind the microphone at the front of the stage to reminisce fondly about his days as the vocalist on Deep Purple's first three albums, harsh reality swiftly put me right. There was to be no re-emergence of the lost singer that night.

In fact, Mark I received remarkably short shrift all evening; if they were mentioned at all, I must have missed it, and even 'Hush' was greeted as a generic Deep Purple song of no particular 'mark' rather than what it actually is, the means by which Evans and Simper, among others, kick-started the band's career, to the benefit, either direct or indirect, of many of those on that stage.

It seemed, again, that Mark I were being written out of history...but that, at least, gave me an opportunity to sort-of shoehorn them back in by getting the Good Old Boys, featuring Nick Simper, into a studio to record some material, both old and new.

The Sunflower Jam was another event that reinforced my determination. I would not allow those grand old rockers to disappear from sight!

10—River Deep, Mountain High

OBSESSION IS AN important part of being a hardcore fan. It is also a major reason for there being few, if any, proper hardcore female fans. In my experience, such as it is, women do not tend to obsess. Not in the same way that men do, at least. They fixate, certainly, but that is not quite the same thing as obsessing. If you want to be a hardcore fan, you have to obsess, genuinely, blokily obsess, about whatever it is of which you are a fan.

Football generates more than its fair share of obsessive fans. Their obsession can manifest itself in a variety of ways. At one end of the spectrum we have such well known examples as John Anthony Portsmouth Football Club Westwood, whose deed poll-altered name is probably the most sober aspect of his obsession. Less spectacular, but every bit as obsessive, there are people like my friend Tosh. His knowledge of football is, quite frankly, freakish. Ask him any question you like about his beloved game and he will supply an answer without missing a beat. I suppose it could all be an elaborate bluff; since his questioner is unlikely to be anywhere near as learned on the subject as he is, he could be saying anything, secure in the knowledge that he will not be found out. It never seems that way, though.

The music obsessive will usually take a different approach. Indeed, music obsession is largely synonymous with that other hardcore fan phenomenon, completism. This is essentially the obsessive desire to own absolutely every piece of recorded material, official and unofficial, that the target artist has ever released, or had released on his, her or their behalf. And not just material by the artist, either: contextual material is important, too.

One friend of mine, for example, is a massive Beach Boys fan—to the extent that, if the Beach Boys are not being talked about, he is not listening. His collection of Beach Boys records, tapes and CDs hugely exceeds in scale anything the band themselves have ever put out. He has every release of their albums and singles, he has every remaster and remix, he has recordings of gigs, many, many of which are bootlegs, he has rehearsal tapes and studio outtakes, he has alternate versions, cover versions, instrumental versions…it is to be wondered whether any human being could ever actually live long enough to listen to it all.

Tosh is not dissimilar, in that his collections of the work of The Rolling Stones and Jethro Tull are extensive, to say the very least.

Here again a gender divide comes into play. To illustrate it, here is a slightly fictionalised conversation I had with a former girlfriend as she examined my collection of Deep Purple CDs. For background, you should know that said CDs are always kept in immaculate condition and so, throughout this conversation, I can be assumed to be in a state of considerable nervous agitation as she picks them up one at a time and looks at them.

She: Why have you got so many live CDs?

Me: They're different gigs.

She: But the songs are all the same!

Me: That's not quite true. Besides, they're by different marks. Careful with that one!

She: Marks? What are you on about?

Me: Line-ups.

She: Look—these songs 'Highway Star' and 'Smoke on the Water' are on all of them.

Me: Well, not the Mark I and early Mark II gigs.

[To be fair, though, this caveat aside, she is more or less right; I could spend several days of my life plugged into my iPod just listening to different versions of the two songs she has named.]

She: I've got no idea what you're talking about.

Me: The band plays them differently at different gigs.

She: Why? Can't they play their instruments properly or something?

Me: No, I explain with increasing impatience, they are superb musicians, but they like to improvise and...

...that's as far as I need to go since she has by now lost interest and moved on to something else.

Completism, it should be clear, is a very real issue and one that can be extremely expensive. Record companies long ago got wise to it and that is why 'remasters' and 'special editions' of classic albums constantly appear in the shops, or, as is more likely to be these days, on Amazon. It has to be said that Deep Purple are by no means innocent on this score. As long ago as the mid-nineties, they, or, rather, their record companies aided and abetted by them, started to put out remasters of all their old albums.

On many levels, this was a welcome development. As Ian Gillan has said, music that was originally engineered and mastered for (quite possibly mono) vinyl albums tends to sound tinny and wishy washy on CD, making a sprucing up of the original tapes something of a necessity. The re-release programme also allowed rarities and previously unreleased tracks to finally see the light of day. At least one song that had never been released before was included on a 'new' version of a Deep Purple album. Mark I's oeuvre benefited as much as any other in that all three of their albums were re-released with a whole raft of rarities and live versions appended to the original track listing (indeed, some of the chapter headings for this very book reference such 'bonus tracks').

That said, because the band's work has been rejigged and re-

released, I—and, I would imagine, many another hardcore fan—have been forced into a position in which I now own two copies of the same album. In the case of those that I first owned on vinyl or cassette, it is more than two copies. I use the word 'forced' here advisedly; remember that we are hardcore fans.

It does not stop there. The tendency of the band—or people associated with it—to record gigs and release them as live albums means that, every few months, it becomes obligatory to shell out yet more precious pounds to acquire the new 'Live in Montreux' or a full gig from the latest Australian tour or whatever.

It does not even stop there. Some years back, the revamped Purple Records decided to gather together as many of the bootleg live recordings from all marks that had been floating around for years as they could, clean them up and issue them 'officially'. These moments in history, which gloried in such titles as 'Kneel and Pray' and 'Perks and Tit', were made available in deliberately basic digipacks and had to be ordered online. Although the performances they immortalise are mostly excellent, the recording quality often leaves much to be desired and few of the gigs are complete. In some cases, not only are the gigs fragmentary, but individual songs are, too.

Nevertheless, owning all of these became a must for me and, as they were released one by one, I dutifully put in my orders and was unable to prevent myself staring like a wide-eyed kid at each one as I carefully unwrapped it before placing it, for the first time, into my CD player.

The same obsessiveness has led me to some of my more inexplicable moments of hardcore fanness. For an example of this, picture me some twenty years ago on a road trip with my ex-wife. In fact, many of my memories of my marriage are of road trips, since it was an activity in which my ex-wife and I engaged with great frequency. Our strategy was simple: we would get over to the European continent with our car and then head off—somewhere. We ended up in a good number of far flung places. On the occasion of relevance to this story, we had made it as far as Avignon in the south of France.

It was a sunny day, but, despite that, we made our customary visit to the local branch of FNAC, which is a sort of continental HMV, i.e. a shop that sells all the sort of stuff you might actually want to buy, such as music, films, hi-fi equipment and the cooler, more 'street cred', books. I was—obviously—looking through 'D' on the CD racks in search of any Deep Purple material that I might not already own, a situation that would only pertain in the event of a title having received no UK release.

My search was perfunctory, as the chances of finding something new were infinitesimally small. But, as I flipped forward a couple of CD jewel cases as a conjurer might flip playing cards, it appeared, magically, in front of me. A white cover design emblazoned with a stylised saxophone, keyboard and a musical note. It didn't look very heavy rock, but the band's name was there, proud and prominent. What was this unexpected treasure?

It was only when I spotted the words 'Jazz Tribute To...' at the top of the picture that I realised what I had. It was not a release by the band, but a collection of jazz covers of Deep Purple songs by the 'Air Jazz Quartet'.

My initial thought was that this was an essential purchase. But then I pulled back. The price, while hardly a banker's bonus, was quite high (and still quoted in Francs back then). My ex-wife and I were young, not especially wealthy and those road trips had to be carefully budgeted: there was scant room for impulse buys. My ex-wife, to her eternal credit, was more bullish, urging me to splash the cash and take home a unique souvenir. I refrained, telling myself that I could always pick the CD up on a different occasion.

On this count, I proved to be stupendously wrong. The album was not available in the UK, neither did I find it on several subsequent trips to France, even during a return visit to the Avignon FNAC. I searched the Internet for it, or, rather, I searched the more primitive version of the Internet that we all lived with in the mid- to late-nineties. I became (let's say it) obsessive in my attempts to get hold of that album. I almost literally searched rivers deep and mountains high.

All to no avail. The Jazz Tribute seemed to have simply vanished—to the extent, in fact, that I began to doubt whether I had ever seen it at all. I questioned my memory. Had I really found the album on one of those road trips, or was it simply something I had dreamed?

Then, courtesy of the ever-giving Internet, it re-appeared. I was looking at one of the fansites that have featured in this narrative (I forget which) and there it was! A whole feature covered the album, saying what it was and what had prompted its recording. There were even a few sound extracts from the tracks. The site supplied details of how to obtain a copy—essentially from Air Jazz Quartet directly—but the instructions on how to do so seemed a little over-complicated and involved supplying credit card details to persons unknown, so I decided for a second time not to go ahead. At this point a good decade had passed since I had first found the CD in that remote branch of FNAC.

This whole anecdote has a sort-of happy ending in that all of the tracks from the Jazz Tribute are now available, in their entirety and without charge, to stream online. I have played them and enjoy them, although it has to be said that the connections to Deep Purple are slight, amounting to little more than a jazzy version of a riff leading into an improvisation that has no discernible connection to the source music.

Completism, then. It's not just a desire to own everything by the band, but everything even vaguely connected to the band. I suppose my interest in the Good Old Boys was an aspect of my completism: in that instance, it was a desire to see the story of Nick Simper completed that spurred me on.

My Rod Evans quest was also motivated by completism, but completism of a more ambitious kind...there is a 'however', of course, and it comes courtesy of this book's great antagonist, time.

Adrian Jarvis

The Jazz Tribute anecdote focuses on obsessiveness, yes, but there is a subtext and this it is: that other things get in the way of obsessiveness, that the concentration wanes, matters start to drift.

The mundane takes over. Ordinariness.

Ultimately, even the dedicated hardcore fan is forced to compromise because he is devoting too much of his energy to the struggle against the passing of the years that we call life.

11—Help!

LIFE, JOHN LENNON said, is what happens while you make your plans.[1] I am not a professional seeker of lost persons and neither am I a full time writer (it's a lucky few who are) and so life carried on happening to me and, as these things do, the quest to find Rod Evans receded into the background. I half-heartedly thought about what I could do to continue with it, but there always seemed to be more pressing claims on my time, like earning a living, travelling, maintaining relationships and other—you know—stuff. The Sunflower Jam gig notwithstanding, I pretty much gave up on the whole thing. I made very little progress on my plans vis-a-vis the Good Old Boys either. Then something wholly unexpected and rather wonderful occurred.

I was idly having a look at The Highway Star website when I noticed that one of its news items went under the title, 'Chasing Shadows'. Intrigued, I clicked on it, expecting a story about that particular song—a cover version by some band or other, perhaps, or an old clip on YouTube of it being performed, either by Purple or, more likely, Nasty Habits. Instead, I found an article about, and a hypertext link to, an early draft of the first few chapters of the very book you are now reading.

---

[1] *Before you cross the street take my hand.*
Life is what happens to you while you're busy making other plans.
—John Lennon, Beautiful Boy (Darling Boy)

As post-modern as this is now becoming, be warned that it is about to become more so, so stick with it. This odd turn of events had happened in the following way: having written the tale up to the point of my holding the Good Old Boys gig, I had placed it on a (now defunct) writers' website—and promptly forgotten all about it. It seems that a Deep Purple fan had stumbled across it, sent the information to the editors of The Highway Star and they had decided to feature it, preceding a lengthy extract from it with a very generous introduction. A good selection of comments from users of the site was also included, most of which were highly positive. This is where things become particularly post-modern because here is one such comment, which is effectively a book review within the text of the book being reviewed:

> This is a fabulous piece of writing. The story resonates
> with me in a big way... Reading this transported me back
> to 1974 in Perth, the year and place I discovered the
> band and, soon after, became a Deep Purple freak. What
> a blast!

As ego-boosting as such tributes were, the thread as a whole had the effect of making me once more reconsider the basis of my investigations. A number of the contributors correctly pointed out that, if Evans did not want to be found, who was I—or anyone else, for that matter—to search for him? He may have once been a public figure, but that did not make him public property; he had every right to the kind of private life that almost everyone else takes for granted. Of course, this was very much my own thinking at that stage, but it was interesting to find it echoed by others. Then, though, there was that particular mystery, which the author of another comment articulated:

> It's incredible really that even in this day of global
> communication that Rod has so completely disappeared,

almost the equivalent of a Rock and Roll Witness
Protection Programme.

Indeed. It was tantalising to imagine Rod going about his own
'Lennon life'—working in a hospital possibly, sitting in a bar with a
cold beer, standing around a barbecue in the glorious Californian
sunshine—all in the company of others, friends, colleagues,
lovers—to at least some of whom he must have revealed his past.

There has to have been a scene—let's place it sometime in the
early 1990s—during which, over a drink or dinner, he let slip to a
recently-met companion that he had once had a fairly successful
musical career. It may have been that his interlocutor was a rock fan
who recognised him from old photographs, or was someone whose
curiosity led him or her to query the gaps in Rod's potted
autobiography where the late sixties, early seventies and, in
particular, 1980, should have been. A drink or two might have
loosened Rod's tongue. He might have been doing the whole
'wonder of me' thing to someone he wished to impress. He could
have been shooting down an especially annoying braggart who was
filling the air with boasts about some minor success, one which
would naturally be dwarfed by the revelation that a bona fide rock
star was in the room.

The point is that someone, somewhere, must know, or have
known, Rod Evans for who he once was. Yet, the silence is total.
Or almost, anyway. Yes, I have come across the odd sighting, half-
sighting and near-sighting—and one significant series of
conversations, as I shall come to—but, apart from those, there has
not been one Tweet, one Facebook status update (at least none that
are known about), one email to the DPAS or The Highway Star.

Nothing.

Whoever may have known Evans and been fully aware of his
Deep Purple past has kept the information to themselves. Have they
done so at his request? If so, those Highway Star contributors were
on to something: his desire for privacy had to be respected. But, did

it? There is a deeper question here. It is really a meditation on the nature of fame itself.

It was a meditation I found myself engaging in more and more as I considered Rod Evans and where he might have disappeared to. Specifically, I worried about where fame's cut off point might fall. The question I wrestled with was: does someone stop being famous simply because he or she ceases to be in the public eye? More to the point, can a commentator in all conscience talk about that person as though he or she is a mere abstraction, an aspect of his or her own fame?

At the time I drafted this section of the book, a controversy raged about whether people have the right to be 'forgotten', that is, to have references to themselves and their actions removed from internet search engines. A court ruling against Google had suggested that they do, but, the technological angle aside, it struck me that the same principle could well apply more generally.

I imagined Rod Evans as retired by now and not wanting to draw too much attention to himself. Was I entitled to discuss him, then, and even to use his name in the title of my book? In my darker moments, I went as far as to wonder whether I was leaving myself open to legal action, but dismissed the concern on the grounds that, for the most part, I was doing nothing more than provide a personal take on public domain material. If, however, I was safe legally, was I morally?

To a large extent, the 'Rod Evans' of this book is only very loosely connected to the 'real' Rod Evans, wherever and whoever he may be. My 'Rod Evans' is a fictional construct, a mythical character embodying a certain obsession of mine and who is the gateway through which I have explored a bigger set of ideas.

Moreover, he is not in any meaningful sense the central figure in this story; that would be me. His appearances have largely been mentions of performances or interviews he once gave, the private life that must have occupied most of his time being hardly touched upon.

I am, of course, being horribly disingenuous here. I have speculated quite freely on Evans' mental states and made judgements—often harsh ones—about his accomplishments and abilities. I can hardly claim to be innocent of taking a biased stance.

Herein lies my dilemma: while those remarks deal with a period that came to an end in 1980, the point at which either Rod Evans or 'Rod Evans' voluntarily withdrew from the public eye, they refer to a person who is still—as far as I am aware—very much alive and susceptible of taking whatever offence they may give. It is not enough to say that he signed up for whatever treatment he might subsequently have received the day he set himself up as a rock and roll star because Rod Evans occupies an unusual celebrity space: he is manifestly still famous (the book you are reading is evidence enough of that), but, at the same time, his whereabouts are unknown and he has made no public pronouncement for a whole generation.

Were he to walk brazenly along a street packed with Deep Purple fans, he would stand an excellent chance of not being recognised. Does his self-engineered obscurity therefore cancel my moral permission to talk about his earlier life, or am I simply an historian, writing of a past time using whatever sources are readily to hand? I like to think the latter, but many of those sources were undreamed of by Rod Evans when he started his career; during those fleeting showbiz years, how could he have predicted that the internet would grow to become something akin to the soul of the world? The thing did not exist back then. He must have thought that his public persona would be far more controllable than is possible in our age of information gluttony.

If I am totally honest, I am yet to find an answer to the problem I raise. I can only hope that the book has a warmth to it and a genuine feeling of affection that ameliorates its more barbed words. It is, when all is said and done, a chronicle of love—and what love is without its ructions?

On which point, the Highway Star piece brought home an

important truth that had been at the back of my mind since the start, but which was now beginning to achieve greater prominence: that I was not the only Deep Purple hardcore fan out there and, since my story had evolved into a tale of what it means to be such a thing, there was plenty of mileage in asking other people for their memories and teasing out common themes. I added my own comment to the thread making this request. It received the response I had been hoping for—a deluge of stories from other hardcore fans.

One resonated with my own particularly closely:

> In spring of 1973 I heard Purple for the first time on a Warner Bros. 45RPM record—"'Smoke on the Water" [studio version] on one side, live on the other. That riff did it. I was hooked and absolutely had to find other Deep Purple records. Meanwhile, I, like probably thousands of other kids of that age, made awkward first attempts at trying to imitate that riff on a cheap guitar. After all these years I still make clumsy attempts to imitate Ritchie Blackmore on guitar.
>
> Each successive Purple album I found, bought, traded for, was a new revelation to me. The songcraft, the virtuosity, the attitude, everything was god-like to my young impressionable mind. Sure I had some good Zeppelin, Sabbath, Grand Funk, Nazareth, and BTO records in my collection, but nothing spoke to me like my Deep Purple records. That remains the case today, even though I have over 1500 CDs of all genres of music (metal, jazz, fusion, rock, funk, world, alternative, pop, prog, etc, etc), Deep Purple remains at the pinnacle for me. Always have, always will.
>
> I have been fortunate to see Deep Purple in concert several times reaching all the way back to the Perfect Strangers tour in 1985. I was front row at the Montreal

Forum. It was [as though] I had died and gone to heaven
seeing my heroes perform maybe 10 feet in front of me. I
went home and preserved my concert experience in
handwritten form in a notebook—no such thing as PCs
back then. Unfortunately, that notebook has disappeared
somewhere in the mists of time.'

There was something quite moving about the author's anecdote, so
willingly shared with me. Like him, I have moved on to other
musicians and musical genres, but, like him, I have found dislodging
a much-loved band from their position at the top of the pile to be
not so easy. And, I must admit that, like him, I have learned some
of the riffs on guitar. Although he was clearly older than myself,
there seemed to be a genuine synchronicity in the lives that we had
led. From other comments on the thread, it was clear that this was
not merely a two-way process.

Another contribution—to my surprise—was of more direct
relevance to the quest for Rod Evans:

I will try to make this brief. I met PN at a Steve Morse
solo show right after Purpendicular came out. (met Steve
for the first time that night too). Me and PN became
friends due to our love of DP and Ritchie Blackmore in
particular. A few years before that he was invited to meet
Rod Evans. Rod worked at a Hospital here in Northern
California as a Respiratory Therapist. PN's mom worked
with a nurse who worked at the same hospital as Rod.
Apparently PN's mom who was best friends with this nurse
that worked with Rod, were talking about their kids.
When this woman found out that PN was a music fan, she
said : "You know, I work with a Dr. Evans who used to be
in a band called Deep Purple." Well, a meeting was
arranged and Rod agreed! PN flaked and never showed
up! He regrets it to this day! If I can get him to post here

137

I will. I have got to know him quite well and he is not a liar/bullshitter. I used to invite him over and we would drink some beer and watch DP, Blackmore vids/DVDs all night! He said the best show he ever saw was Rainbow in San Francisco (with Ronnie James Dio) in 1978 and that Ritchie smashed more than one Strat that night!

My initial reaction was that this was a startling new development of potentially game-changing importance. Not only was it the first time that I had come across a possible post-1980 sighting of Evans—albeit reported second or third hand—but, in placing him in the medical profession, it had more than a hint of plausibility about it. It also answered the point about how much the people around him knew of his past. If the comment were to be believed (and why not believe it?) we could infer that Evans was not in the habit of being coy about his pre-medicine days, that he was, in fact, happy to talk about them.

In a strange kind of way, this one simple comment on the Internet gave me more of a connection to Evans as a person than all of the material that I had unearthed from other sources. Through those few brief sentences, I glimpsed a little of Rod Evans the man, the working medic at ease with his achievements in showbiz, but absolutely sure that they belonged to a closed chapter of his life. That imagined scene of mine from the Californian province of Never Really Was now altered to feature a Rod Evans with an indulgent smile and a sense of irony in the face of starry eyed probings from his companions. It was a more likable Rod Evans than I had hitherto conjured up in my mind.

Unfortunately, it got me no nearer to meeting the man himself. Since the comment placed 'PN's' abortive rendezvous with Rod some time before the release of Deep Purple's Purpendicular album, my scene-setting in the early nineties was not too far off the mark. There was still a more than twenty year gap to account for and there was little to fill it apart from occasional titbits thrown up here and there by my research.

One such was the quirky little anecdote relayed to me by Jerry Bloom about a mysterious stranger he met on the night of 31st of May, 1997 in Esbjerg, Denmark. The date and place are so specific because they were where and when the nineties Rainbow played for the last time. Having left Deep Purple soon after that infamous 1993 NEC gig—Ritchie Blackmore reformed his other heavy rock vehicle for one last go before hanging up his fuzz peddle forever, or, at least, for the best part of twenty years. The band played at a festival in the town and, performance over, retired to a hotel for some after-show R and R. Also present were Cozy Powell, the drummer who had been in the line-up that recorded Rising, and Jerry.

At some point, the gathering was crashed by a starstruck Swedish man carrying a huge pile of vinyl LPs. Among them were, of course, Rainbow's complete oeuvre. There were also works by lesser-known artists for whom Blackmore, Powell and any others who might have been staying in that hotel had worked as session musicians. The man explained that he liked to get his records signed by every musician who had played upon them and was quite prepared to make an uninvited guest of himself in order to do so. He was carrying all three Mark I albums.

'You're not going to get the singer's autograph,' Jerry quipped upon spotting them.

The man looked at him knowingly and replied that, on the contrary, he knew someone who had Evans' address and was more than willing to send albums to be signed, a service that Evans was happy to provide. But, as has been so often the case in this tale of Mr. E, the lead was lost when the man disappeared into the night before he could be quizzed further; Jerry never even discovered his name.

Then there was a strange telephone call that Ian Hansford received sometime during the nineties (he was a little unclear about the year). Hansford tells the story best himself:

I'm sitting here and the phone goes; my son gets it and he just starts shouting and shouting and shouting, "Dad! There's this effing rude person on the phone wants to speak to you, won't tell me his name and he's got an American accent". I went, "Hello; who's that?" And he said, "It's Rod. Is Cokey there?"—which is a nickname for my ex-wife. He kept just going on and on and on and I said, "You're wasting my time. What do you want?" and so on and so forth and, "I'm putting the phone down, I've had enough of you".

Two minutes later, it rang again. He wouldn't tell me where he was. I said, "Where you calling from?" He went, "Northern California" and I went, "What, like San Francisco?" He said, "No! NORTHERN California". I think he must have been right up just below Oregon or somewhere like that. He'd remarried and he had two young children, but he wouldn't tell me where he was, he wouldn't give me the phone number and basically I think he had a job and he had use of the phone at night.

I also remember that he was doing the same thing to Chip Hawkes—you know, from The Tremeloes. I think the last time I had seen him was at the Roundhouse when he was in Captain Beyond. Basically, the conversation was that he wanted to speak to Ros ['Cokey'] and he said, "Give me her number". I was like, "I'm not giving you her number; I'm sure she doesn't want to speak to you anyway" and so on and so forth. In the end I was like, "Rod, you're getting on my nerves; if you were in front of me now, I'd put your nose through your brain". "That's more like Bige! That's more like the old Ian!" and this, that and the other, he said. So, basically, that was the last time I had any contact with him.

Entertainingly, Hansford was less concerned with Evans' interest in his ex-wife (with whom Evans had had a relationship during her young, free and single years), than with his affectation of an American accent: his pronunciation of 'Tomato' in the American manner came in for special criticism.

Whether the enigmatic Swedish stranger had a hot line to Evans or whether Evans genuinely wanted to reconnect with Ian Hansford, the question of why members of the missing singer's social circle do not mention him in any traceable medium remains open. Even in the stories I have recounted, it is a colleague of PN's mother who claimed to know Evans and there is no way of ascertaining how truthful were the claims of the man from Esbjerg.

Ian Hansford ended his call having gleaned no clear information as to Evans' whereabouts. Evans remained several degrees of separation from me. As much as he was solidifying slightly in front of me, he was still a shadowy presence, shimmering and insubstantial. Later, much later, another source, a musician, would give me more information than any of these people, but he would do little to make the picture less blurred...if anything, he would only add layers of mystery.

In the meantime, however, another, possibly more fruitful, effect of The Highway Star feature was a renewed desire on my part to get The Good Old Boys into a recording studio. The feature itself was a strong pretext, so I sent the following email to Richard Hudson:

Hi Richard!

Long time, no speak! I'm getting in touch because something I wrote detailing my experiences with early Deep Purple has emerged and been featured on The Highway Star website; I mention it to you since it is as much about The Good Old Boys as anything else (in fact, the narrative movement of the thing might be from searching for Deep Purple to finding the GOBs). It is not finished yet! I thought you might be interested—and maybe could even contribute some stories to it as I strive to finish it.

I also have a proposition for you—admittedly a slightly screwy one. When we spoke at the Beaky Band gig a few months back you mentioned that you had written some original songs for the GOBs but that they had never got around to rehearsing them. I would love to hear them—in fact, I would love to get them recorded. Do you think that it might be possible to persuade the other members of the band to have a shot at this? If I could organise some time in a studio (and that is a big 'if—I might be able to call in some favours, but, then again...), would there be any chance of getting the boys together for a day to lay down, say, two of your new songs together with (availability of recording rights permitting) 'Apache' and 'Hush'? The idea would be to create an 'EP' that could then either be made available through iTunes or burnt on to CDs to sell at your gigs.

Anyway, it's just a thought...I see that the band is touring over the summer: I will do my best to get along to a gig.

With customary promptness and courtesy, Richard got back to me within twenty four hours:

Hi Adrian,
Great to hear from you again. I will certainly look at the Highway Star website, and if there is anything I can add I will contact you.

I like the idea of recording some new songs, but I don't think the band would want to record any new songs that they haven't played and worked on in the act beforehand. I will mention it to them and get their response, as it would be great to have some new material released for sale. I look forward to seeing you at one of the gigs.

Cheers,

Richard

This was not quite the unequivocal 'yes' that I had hoped for, but neither was it an outright rejection of the idea. I was not discouraged. After all, I have consistently characterised my research as a 'quest' and, if quests were easy, the corpus of Arthurian literature (including the original Book of Taliesin, maybe) would be somewhat smaller.

A day or two after this email, I received a call from Richard. I was sitting on Karen's settee at the time doing something that has occupied many hours of my life and, doubtless, many hours of the lives of all men in relationships with women: waiting for her to finish getting ready to go out. On the one hand, I felt honoured to receive a call from him, on the other, I began to feel that he was turning from an almost-friend into a genuine friend.

'Adrian?' he began, a little tentatively.

I was unable to keep the thrill out of my voice: 'Richard! Hi! How are you?'

'Well. And you?'

'Very well! What can I do for you?'

'I had a read of your book.'

'Did you like it?'

'Yes. It was really well written. I don't know if there is anything I can add—or if you need me to add anything. I never really knew Rod Evans.'

I had been broadly aware of this, and had not really expected anything else.

'That's okay. It's not the only thing the book's about.'

'Did you find him?'

'No. No. No-one has. Even the BBC with all their resources couldn't get anywhere, so what chance did I stand?'

'Maybe he's dead!'

This had occurred to me. It is unlikely that he would have got much of an obituary.

'It doesn't really matter—I went looking for Rod Evans, but found the Good Old Boys instead, so it hasn't been a bad journey.'

'That's nice to hear! I like your idea of recording some songs.'

'Excellent! My view is that it would be great to get some of your original material taped and also to make a permanent recordings of some of the numbers that you perform live—'Hush' would be good and your version of 'Apache' is better than The Shadows' original; I think so anyway...'

He was flattered by this, but tried to demur, returning to the theme of getting some material on to tape.

'I would love to get some stuff down,' he said, 'But the original songs would need to be worked up in the set; we would need to see if they were a fit for Alan's voice. Getting the band to rehearse is difficult.'

'Maybe you should introduce the songs into your set!'

'Maybe...'

'I just think that it would be a shame if the band didn't make a permanent record of some of its material—assuming that we can get the recording rights to a couple of the songs, that is.'

His greater experience came in here as he assured me that that would not be a problem. I decided to get down to business:

'If you would like to get into a studio, I would be willing to arrange that—you know, I could broker something. I know a couple of people who could engineer and produce the songs and I might be able to get some studio time.'

'That would be good if you could do it.'

Actually, I was not one hundred percent certain that I could, but this was an occasion when 'can do' had to trump 'yes, but'...'Look,' I said, 'Let's keep in touch and try to work this out.'

'Yes, we should,' he replied, adding, 'and I'll show your work to Nick and see what he thinks.'

This was a result beyond my most optimistic imaginings. We exchanged a few more pleasantries and then rang off.

Karen had entered the room by now and had witnessed my side of the conversation with a stance that began as bemused, before turning to comprehension as she realised who my interlocutor was, only to end up as excitement at the prospect of taking the Good Old Boys project further.

Of course, once I had pressed the red telephone icon on the touch-sensitive screen that was my gateway to everywhere, a realisation of the obligation I had just placed myself under began to dawn. Just where was I going to find a recording studio and—equally importantly—a producer?

My first idea was to tap up my claimed contacts. In truth—as I probably do not need to say—these amounted to a couple of Facebook friends and—as I probably also do not need to say—nothing came of them. Karen had the idea of taking advantage of one of the many offers that pop up on those deal websites that let people get vouchers for all manner of disconnected goods and services and on which, occasionally, a recording studio advertises a two hour or half day session for a hundred pounds or so. Such places, though, too often only pander to the vanity of deluded X-Factor wannabes; they are not fit places for musicians of The Good Old Boys' calibre to do their thing. Besides, if that was all I was going to bring to the table, then why was I needed in the first place? No. I had to be sure to engineer an opportunity for the band that no-one else could. But how?

One answer was staring me in the face. I did, as it happens, know someone who owned a recording studio—or, rather, had a recording studio in his basement—and it was someone with whom I had worked before.

To explain this, we need to head back to the late nineties, to that pre-millennium, pre-9/11 world in which everything seemed so much simpler (or maybe that's just my memory of it). I was writing a musical with a friend, colleague and collaborator of mine.

My contribution was at the words end of things: I was hammering out the script and lyrics, while he composed the music.

Neither of us had done anything remotely like this before. Were I to attempt such a project now, I would no doubt be daunted by the scale of it; to write a straight play is to master the art of keeping multiple balls in the air, all of which are not, in fact, ball-shaped (which would be relatively easy) but jagged, cumbersome, awkward and non-standard in design. Add songs to the mix—original songs at that—and the labour becomes close to mind-boggling, especially when the songs' composers are only composers because they say they are and take on their creative work with no particular reason to expect that they can complete it. But, we were—if not exactly kids—much younger men who were prepared to face down a challenge, however crazy. We were sure of our talents and armed with a nuclear arsenal of self-belief.

The piece itself was, in retrospect, a strange mixture of ideas. I wanted to create a musical version of Fritz Lang's classic 1926 film Metropolis. There were only two snags with this concept; the first was that we would need to get permission to do it and the second was that such permission would probably be withheld because the film had been unsuccessfully adapted into a musical once before. Nevertheless, we pressed on, putting together an original play set in a Year 2000 as it might have been imagined from the 1930s (it was a vision that bore more than a passing resemblance to the world of Metropolis). The approach allowed my friend to indulge his love of the music of Kurt Weill and he wrote some lovely songs in that style. Conceptually somewhat bizarre, the whole thing kind-of worked, and, when we showcased it at a theatre in Birmingham, we earned a few plaudits and even some positive press reviews.

The one point on which everyone who had taken part agreed was that the songs had been entertaining and memorable, or, at least, memorable enough to merit preservation beyond the run of the show. We therefore decided to ensure that permanent, definitive versions be stored on DAT tape for posterity, albeit that the untrained voices of some cast members led to the label 'definitive' being a little inappropriate in a few cases. One of the play's leads (who has gone on to greater showbiz things since) was the son of a musician whose jobs had included playing keyboards with a couple of successful 1980s bands. He was the guy with the studio, which, along with his time, he willingly donated. Thanks to him, we all spent a happy Saturday laying down the vocals against pre-recorded backing tracks.

Given this history, I hoped that he might be open to letting us use his facilities and, if he felt so inclined, to engineering and producing the recordings too. His wife—a successful actress in her own right—was a Facebook friend and so I sent her a message, mooting the possibility of getting the recordings done:

> *Right—now this is going to seem unbelievably cheeky, so please feel free to tell me to bugger right off (although don't 'defriend' me—I'm not going to be THAT obnoxious), but I was wondering if you still have your recording studio and, if so, if you would be interested in getting involved with a little pet project of mine?*
>
> *The story is that—for all sorts of reasons that it would be easier to tell you verbally—I have become involved with a band of old time rockers who tour under the name of The Good Old Boys. They all have distinguished histories. One is Richard Hudson, erstwhile member of The Strawbs and Hudson-Ford; another is Nick Simper, former bass player with Deep Purple; others have been in bands like Warhorse and Renaissance. Anyway, they are amazing live and I think that it would be great—and quite sweet, really—to get them into a studio to record a few of their tracks which could then be made available via iTunes (my thinking is that it would perhaps be four—two of Richard Hudson's original songs and two cover versions). To that end, I am trying to source*

a studio and a bit of time in which to record some stuff—
and a producer (hint hint). This is all at an early stage—
I have spoken to Richard about it, but he is yet to broach
it with the rest of the band, so this is all very tentative.
Nevertheless, do you think you might be interested? If
nothing else, this would be a chance to preserve some
really fine music by a bunch of old guys who really know
how to rock!'

I was pleased when she got back to me almost immediately, saying
that it could be interesting and that she would certainly mention it
to her husband. This was very promising indeed! But, I was still a
long way from being in a position to press the 'go' button....

12—We Can Work It Out

'I STILL CAN'T believe you know JK! It's incredible! To meet you here—of all places!'

As a quotation, this needs a little explaining. The 'here' was Ghent in Belgium. Normally a sleepy medieval town characterised by some beautiful architecture of the type that appears a lot in the backgrounds of paintings by Vermeer, for ten days each year it becomes one of the playgrounds of Europe as it holds a festival that is an orgy of music, drinking and over-indulgent eating. Fried stuff-selling kiosks and beer-soaked temporary bars spring up all over the place, while the permanent cafes and restaurants enjoy bumper takings.

Performance stages of various sizes are erected in every available space—squares (obviously), as well as courtyards, the entrances of buildings and even the bank of a canal (a novel location that necessitates most of the audience standing a whole waterway removed from the show they are watching). The acts are mostly local covers bands—versions of The Good Old Boys, maybe—who are, more often than not, professional-sounding and fun to listen to. Not, it must be said, that the quality of the music much matters, since, by the time the nightly party is in full swing, most festival-goers are too booze-addled to notice.

I was in Ghent as part of a road trip (yes, another one of those) with a friend from university. By this point in the narrative, such journeys had become an almost annual event. Previous adventures had seen us drive different classic sports cars all the way through France, down the entire length of Italy and around Sicily, as well as through the centre of Spain from extreme north to coastal south.

This time, we were following a circuit covering Belgium, Germany and Switzerland, stopping off at different towns en route and getting together with any members of our circle who happened to be there at the same time or who lived in the vicinity. At a guesthouse in Switzerland, for example, we found ourselves talking with our hostess about the Swiss origins of Deep Purple's Machine Head and Burn albums and, of course, 'Smoke on the Water', which chronicles the destruction by fire of the casino in Montreux, a town 'on the Lake Geneva shoreline'.

The journey began with us joining a group of my friend's friends who had converged on Ghent for a taste of the festival. A member of this motley crue was the speaker of the above line. He was called Simon and he was one of those people with the gift of making you feel like you have known him forever within about thirty seconds of first meeting him. The 'JK' to whom he was referring was a former pupil of mine who had left school some years earlier. JK had been a committed 'techie' at school; that is, he had been part of the team that provided sound and lighting for school shows and events. He had worked with me on a number of drama productions and even played the drums in the band for a musical based around 1980s songs that I had once directed.

The connection between Simon and JK was that the former was in the process of building a recording studio in which the latter worked as engineer (while completing a degree in sound and lighting design). More remarkably, the studio was within half an hour's drive of where I was living. Hence the amazed tone of Simon's words. Between the Highway Star article and this bizarrely co-incidental meeting, I was beginning to think that someone up there wanted me to complete my quest—or, at any rate, some sort of quest.

My friend, my friend's friends and I had, as a group, gone out for dinner before losing ourselves in the swirling crowds that filled the picturesque streets. It was at this point, while clutching a plastic cup of fizzy Belgian beer that I had broached to Simon the possibility of using his studio to lay down some Good Old Boys material.

I felt the need to do this because the enquiry to my past collaborator had—perhaps predictably—failed to elicit a positive response. Or a response of any kind, to be honest. I could hardly blame her. After all, what I was asking was quite a big favour—I had not mentioned a payment in my original email. She was a busy woman. If her Facebook page was to be believed (and, since it was emblazoned with supporting photographs, it was pretty convincing), she spent much of her time travelling, partly in support of her increasingly busy son and partly in pursuit of her own acting interests. It was no real surprise that my out-of-the-blue request had slipped from her mind.

It was thus with some eagerness that I had heard of Simon's recording studio project. Having mentioned to him the idea of using his facilities, we agreed that they could be made available ahead of their formal opening for a considerably reduced rate. Hardly had the last beer been supped that rainy festival night before I emailed Richard with the news that the notion of recording some original Good Old Boys material might become a reality. As was usual, he replied almost immediately, saying that he would discuss my proposal with the band.

There was little else that I could do for the next few days. I spent a good portion of them in the passenger seat of an open-top sports car chewing up the roads of Central Europe at crazily high speeds. With spooky, or serendipitous, timing, I received a call from Richard as soon as the road trip ended.

'Hi Richard!' I said as his name came up on my smartphone.

'Adrian! How are you?' came the calm, generous voice at the other end of the line.

I replied that I was fine and, the pleasantries over, he told me why he was calling: 'I spoke to the band about your idea of recording some new material...'

'Were they in favour?'

'They thought it was an excellent idea, but, like me, they thought it would be best to record something new, some new songs.'

'I agree! It was you telling me that you had written some new songs that put the idea into my head in the first place.'

'I told them about you—they were amazed and quite moved that there was someone out there taking that kind of interest.'

I felt very happy at this. He continued: 'We think that we should record an album, but new stuff. We've put out three live albums before now and they contain everything we play—I think the Shadows' track, "Apache", is about the only thing that's not on a record.'

'So you're going to rehearse some of your songs?'

'Yes, but I'd like to get the band together to do some writing, create some new stuff for an album.'

This was exactly what I had hoped for—to see these guys doing what they used to do, and do so well.

'It's difficult, though,' he went on, 'a couple of the guys have still got jobs. They work during the week and in the evenings you just want to relax, so organising a session isn't easy.'

'What about the recording?'

I was already planning to tell Simon that we wanted to pencil in such-and-such a date to do some recording. Richard had a surprisingly different take: 'Well, a couple of the guys know someone in London who owns a studio—which is better for us, obviously—and there are some very good engineers there who are also musicians, so they will be able to really get the sound right.'

In some respects, of course, this piece of news was tantamount to my redundancy notice; what role was left for me if the band was able to organise everything themselves? Strangely, I didn't see it that way, and neither did Richard. He said: 'Thank you for everything you've done. You've really got us moving with this.'

That was the point, I suppose. My involvement was always going to be primarily motivational. I was there to make the band believe in themselves, to let them know that someone was listening. That is what it means to be a hardcore fan. There is nothing wrong with that. In fact, there is everything right with it: in its own way, it is a vital part of the process.

'The band has been drifting a bit,' Richard said, 'so it's good to have something to aim for. I would really like to get them together to write some new material. They can all do it.'

'That's what I want,' I said, 'I just want to hear the new songs! So, can I ask two things?'

He assented.

'Could you let me know when you debut any songs at a gig, because I would love to hear them live.'

'Of course!'

'And—would you mind if I popped along to a recording session, so I can write about it?'

'I was going to say. We'd love to have you along. You've got us going on this and it's a fresh pair of ears.'

'Brilliant!'

'I'll try to get the others together—if I haven't been in touch in about a month, send me something to get me moving!'

'Absolutely! I'll email you a clipart picture of a boot to remind you to give everyone a kick up the arse! Yes—if you need a "fixer", I'll be it!'

The conversation strayed into some more trivial areas before we hung up.

I was in my car and had pulled into a lay-by to take the call. For several minutes, I sat with a large, silly grin on my face as the indifferent 'whoosh' of cars speeding past me faded away, irrelevant to my reverie.

You've read enough of this now to have guessed that, over the next few weeks, nothing really happened. Everyone was too busy and maybe it was wrong of me to expect too much of these old men who just wanted to enjoy what by rights should have been a well-earned retirement.

I sent Richard the threatened 'kick-up-the-arse' email nearly three months later. With customary promptness and courtesy, he called, leaving me a voice mail message, the gist of which was that he had tried to get the Boys together to jam some new songs—he had even offered them a financial inducement—but to no avail. There was simply too little enthusiasm, too many other commitments, too much in the way.

Nothing had happened.

Indeed, Richard had pretty much given up on the idea. The new Good Old Boys album, then, was dead, or rather, stillborn, or, rather, never conceived in the first place. There would be no fresh material and, neither, it seemed, would my quest have an ending.

13—Love Help Me

THE MAJOR DIFFERENCE between fiction and non-fiction is the author's degree of control. Were this a novel, the plot would now move towards a climax in which the Good Old Boys record some wonderful new songs that make them all feel like they're twenty five years old again, while I hug Karen amidst some inanely cheesy dialogue with my new friend Richard as a sagacious and benign mentor figure in the background. That is how the romantic comedy film based on this book will end.

As should be clear by now, though, this narrative is not nearly so neat—for all the fictionalisation that has inevitably gone into its telling. In rock music terms, it is less like a four minute studio version than a lengthy improvisation-heavy live run through; it is, to give an example, not so much the well-mannered version of 'Hush' from 'Shades of Deep Purple' as the messy account of that song that ended the Celebrating Jon Lord Sunflower Jam.

An even better analogy might be with the Air Jazz Quartet's Deep Purple tributes, which only really have much to do with the band at the start, the bulk of any given track being a series of extemporisations remote from the genre of rock music, let alone anything ever produced by Messieurs Blackmore, Lord and Co. This story has followed a similar line: it began by being all about Deep Purple, but they have faded into the background somewhat as my quest has developed into more of a personal journey. In short, I went looking for a mythical Rod Evans, but found a very real

Richard Hudson.

It was a telephone conversation with Richard that opened up some intriguing new possibilities in the wake of the disappointment surrounding the proposed Good Old Boys recordings. I learned that he had, in fact, been working on some original material, but, rather than being for the band, it was for a putative solo project.

The idea—about which Richard sounded very excited—was to produce a concept album on the life of Charles Darwin. I asked if there would be any singing or quotations from Darwin's works, but, apart from one track that would probably include some female vocals, it was to be entirely instrumental. The recordings were planned for a studio in Luxembourg. It all sounded highly intriguing and Richard's promise to send me some demos when they became available was certainly something to look forward to.

As it happened, I didn't have to wait too long. A day or two later, I received an email from Richard containing an MP3 file. It was not, however, anything to do with a certain nineteenth century naturalist, but a demo of a more conventional song that he had written.

I hesitated before opening the link. I felt exactly as I had just before I first met Nick Simper: what if it was a total let down? Would my illusions be shattered? It was with some nervousness that I hovered the pointer over the file's icon and clicked.

The song was called 'Mean Evil Loving Man', which, as a title, is undoubtedly attention-grabbing, combining the promise of down 'n' dirty bluesy rock and roll with a nice sense of humour. The music began with a driving guitar riff overlaid with some brassy synthesiser chords that it could easily be imagined might be replaced by actual horns in a definitive recording.

When the vocals kicked in, though, it was obvious that this was a rock song to the core; it was crying out for the kind of rapid-fire, twinkle-in-the-eye, growly-voiced screaming that is the core trade of any good rock front man. With a couple of guitar solos and a clever use of those brass stabs to create a sinister underpinning to the main riff, 'Mean Evil Loving Man' was not only a classic in the making, but, by rights, a rock and roll standard. It is the mark of quality in a song that it can sound like it's been around for years on first listening: this one accomplished that in spades. I immediately got back to Richard expressing my admiration.

The title of Richard's song could have been a chapter heading for a written up account of the next bit of information I received about Mr. E himself.

Like much of what I was learning about him, it came from a surprising source, someone with whom my path crossed by pure chance. It happened that I was contacted by a certain Maria, who had picked up on my research through Facebook and was keen to impart to me her story. Unfortunately, in that she was Italian, lived in an Italian city and spoke only Italian, the details came through falteringly and over a considerable period of time, giving the whole thing the air of a rather soapy daytime TV serial. Whatever translation software she was using proved its lack of worth by turning some of her words into bizarre English sentences that needed another level of interpretation before they could be made to mean anything. The photographs that she sent, however, were eloquent indeed.

According to Maria, she entered the scene in 1967 when The Maze had a short residency at a theatre in Milan providing music for a stage play. Ian Paice spoke of this episode in a relatively recent interview (although he mentioned only 'the band', the timings suggest that he must have been referring to The Maze).

Maria told me that she was working in a department store opposite and one day caught the eye of a number of 'guys' hanging around the stage door. One of them made a special connection with her and, like someone in a rom-com montage, turned up at her counter for three days in a row on flimsy pretexts before finally having the courage to ask her out. He revealed that those 'guys' had been the members of The Maze and he was the lead singer. She responded to his overtures by swiftly dropping her current boyfriend and beginning what sounded like a fairly intense affair conducted through a barrier of mutual linguistic misunderstanding. She did learn his name, though: Rod Evans. She described him to me as 'a fascinating guy, very polite, soft-spoken', who, 'acted as a big brother to Ian Paice which [sic] was much more shy and they were always together'.

She claimed that Evans talked about marrying her, but had to return to England with the band at the completion of the play's run. Happily for her, that development was not terminal for the relationship, which continued via letters, excerpts from which Maria shared with me in photographic form. The ones supposedly from Evans were rendered in a neat, but florid, hand and had a sincere, honest tone that would have tended to confirm Maria's story if they could have been verified.

But the photographs were a little inconclusive on that point and, moreover, I was troubled by the fact that one of them had clearly been dated by someone else, someone Italian judging by the spelling of the month. I wondered why that had been done: perhaps to prove the authenticity of the letter? If so, it had exactly the opposite effect, being an anomalous addition that had me doubting its provenance.

Evans, I was told, asked to spend Christmas 1967 with Maria and her family, but she put him off, saying that a large number of relatives would be there and that there would be no space for him too. In fact, as she confided in me, she was reluctant to let him see the rather modest circumstances in which she and her family lived.

Had that been the whole story, it would have been the tiniest of footnotes, a conventional anecdote about a young girl duped by a rock star who, having strung her along for a while, got back to a life of which she could never hope to be a part.

But that was not the whole story. Maria told me of how she was not so easily cast aside, embarking instead on an epic, perhaps foolhardy, journey to the UK which took her, in the first instance, to Slough in search of Evans and his family. She had little or no

English, hardly any money and nobody to turn to if everything went wrong. She freely admitted that she had been naïve and scared, not knowing what to do or how to behave; she said that, on one occasion, she even ate dog food, believing it to be something more palatable.

Heading next to London, (she said) she got together with Evans and kept him company during the recording of The Book of Taliesyn, the two of them spending the evenings in town, frequenting a pub that was popular with other recording artists and megastars of the future, such as Rod Stewart, The Hollies and Eric Clapton. I pictured this soi disant golden couple disappearing into Time Magazine's famous 'Swinging London' cover like a pair of cut out cartoon figures, ageless and free, backed by a soundtrack of wah-wah guitars and oompahing horns.

Following her return to Milan, Maria told me that she received a letter from Evans formally proposing marriage, to which she agreed. A second letter went to her parents since, at the age of twenty, she was, under Italian law, unable to marry without their consent. A further letter of October 1968, dated just a few days before Deep Purple embarked on a large scale tour of the USA, gave instructions regarding the organization of the wedding.

Then, one hurried Trans-Atlantic telephone call notwithstanding, everything went quiet. Maria told me that she did not hear anything from Evans for over a month. She wrote to his mother, but the reply that came back simply said that he was very busy; by this stage, 'Hush' had become a hit in America and the single version of 'Kentucky Woman' was also doing well. It seems that Evans disappeared from Maria's life, much as he has disappeared from the world at large.

The coda is that she only discovered that Evans had met someone else in America years later when she read a biography of Ritchie Blackmore. Movingly, she wrote to me: 'Adrian all my life I wanted to close the circle of this story. At least before the end of life, I wish with all my heart to talk to Rod' [sic]. Don't we all, I thought.

The lack of photographic evidence for any of this was something that Maria herself lamented and it certainly led to my applying a critic's eye to the story. I wondered why none of this had ever come out before, since it sounded like the plot of a fair-to-middling fictional potboiler.

Ian Hansford confirmed that Evans met his first wife in the USA, although he was unable to say whether it had been on the particular tour that featured in Maria's story. I also bore in mind what Ian had said about Evans having, 'an eye for the ladies'. Was Maria merely one of many? She may have had an unusually strong connection to Evans, but she was anything but unique.

The single 'Emmaretta', (recorded at around the time of the Third Album, but still concurrently with Maria's story) was said to have been inspired by Evans' passion for Emmaretta Marks from the cast of Hair. It seemed strange that he would write such a thing if he had been in love with another all along. That said, with lyrics focused on letter writing—the activity through which much of his relationship with Maria had, she said, taken place—and a title that, at least in its first half, could be someone spelling out the name 'Maria', I briefly fancied that it might instead have been about my Italian correspondent.

Whatever the truth, Maria's story did nothing to get me closer to finding Evans, although it did help me to form a sharper mental image of what he might have been like as a person. She described him as something of a romantic, exciting to be around, and with a good deal of depth. A less charitable opinion might have followed from his behaviour towards the end of the alleged affair, but Maria's refusal to condemn was a feature of her narrative.

I don't know whether telling me what happened helped her to 'close the circle', but I hoped that she felt a little better for it. I did need to remind myself that what she said was only her side of things and, in spite of the 'documents' that she produced, could well have better reflected a young woman's fantasies than what really took place; Evans may have had a very different take, had he been around to give it. Another source, not this time Italian, but German, was later to give me an alternative view of him, one that was intended to clear up mysteries, but which actually did no more than add whole new layers to them.

Still, while Maria was taking me back into her past lives, my life in the present was continuing and, at the same time as engaging in such research, I was busy putting on a production of the musical We Will Rock You, which is based on songs by Queen.

Up to that point, I had never really liked Queen, if I'm honest. I had always found them a bit too camp, a bit too arch, a bit too—well—soft. I should not by now need to emphasise that this is the chronicle of a love affair with heavy rock and roll. Harmonies, synthesisers, disco-y beats and the like had never really been my thing.

Working on the show, though, gave me an entirely new perspective. I began to realise that there was genuine wit in the songs and, yes, the harmonies and long notes were all part of their overall effect. They certainly worked in the context of the show; when sung with different voices, chorus backings and in arrangements that favoured the bombastic, they came alive in all their over-the-top glory. I invited Richard to come along to see a performance—bearing in mind that reaching my part of East Anglia from London was not that quick or easy an undertaking.

As a whole, We Will Rock You is perhaps most interesting in what it says about the politics of rock music. It supposedly takes place in a sort-of dystopian future, albeit one that is so lightly imagined that it barely differs from the present. Elements of The Matrix, 1984 and a host of other messianic sci-fi stories are brought into the tale of a 'Dreamer' who, it is prophesied, will lead the world away from bland commercialism towards a new age of self-expression, inspired by the spirits, if not the actual minds and bodies, of the members of Queen themselves.

It struck me as odd that this nonsense—entertaining nonsense for sure, but nonsense all the same—had been written by, of all people, Ben Elton. Once very firmly a 'trendy lefty' member of the Comic Store circle, Elton had never been coy about his socialist politics and, yet, We Will Rock You celebrates individualism. The Dreamer character, 'Galileo', sings of wanting to break free and his desire to make music is explicitly denounced by the main villain as 'the act of an individual'.

Is rock music about individualism? It's certainly populated by rebel rebels, street fighting men and speed kings who are running wild and free. But it demands conformism to a beat and many of its ideas and assumptions are numbingly simplistic. As political and social commentary, it is not particularly deep.

Nowhere is this starker than in the ways that it talks about women who, frankly, do not come out of it very well. For a start, they all seem to be called 'Susie' (although, for balance, it should be pointed out a high number of male characters in rock songs are called 'Johnny'). More seriously, rock songs are, in general, insultingly reductive about the individual natures and social roles of women. Deep Purple, it must be said, are major offenders in this regard. Songs like 'Strange Kind of Woman', 'Mitzi Dupree' and 'Lady Luck' are explicitly about prostitutes and it is hard to think of too many occasions on which anything like romance makes an appearance. 'Woman From Tokyo' and 'Fireball' are two odd exceptions as are, interestingly, several Mark I numbers, such as 'Emmaretta' and 'Blind'.

Otherwise, Deep Purple's lyrics tend to portray women in a strictly two dimensional way. In this, they are definitely not alone. "Mean Evil Loving Man'—for all the fact that Richard clearly wrote it with his tongue superglued to the inside of his cheek—is spoken by the character of a man who sleeps with women but offers them no love.

To a large extent, historical attitudes are at work here. Most of the music that has featured in these pages was written in the late sixties and early seventies, a time when sexual politics were clearly somewhat less complex than they are now.

Maria's story gives a hint of that: it is so rooted in a specific historical context that it would be impossible to transpose it intact to a more recent setting. Her odyssey to London would, for a start, be rendered unnecessary by the existence of smartphones and social media sites and who asks a woman's parents for her hand in marriage anymore? Where I have alluded to music that post-dates that time, much of it has been written in the same idiom and so preserves many of the same old prejudices and assumptions in fossil form.

That attitudes have changed since those far off, fading days can perhaps best be illustrated by the music of David Coverdale's Deep Purple spin-off band Whitesnake. There are moments, many, many moments, when this little lot's output is eye-wateringly sexist, going on, as it does, about 'skinny little girls' in 'tight-ass jeans' and men who 'ride' women with hearts 'as cold as ice'.

It is one of the less comfortable aspects of rock music that its politics are so retrograde and unprogressive. Protest songs are comparatively rare, although far, as we have seen, from non-existent. The type of individualism and freedom for which rock songs voice a yearning is conceived of in straightforward terms. It is an escape from authority or the avoidance of punishment by the law. Often, it is expressed through the evocation of puerile fantasy worlds. Seldom is it an engagement with the pressing issues of the day.

We Will Rock You, the musical, attempts to address this problem. The lead female character, 'Scaramouche', constantly rails against being labelled 'chick', a term which the faux rockers of the twenty fourth century mistakenly believe indicates respect. She is also the most functionally intelligent character on the stage, the nominal hero living up to his 'dreamer' billing in being ineffectual and lacking in obvious talent.

I was midway through rehearsals for the show when Richard called to clarify a couple of issues.

'I just want to give you some background to the demo I sent you,' he said.

'I really love it!' I told him.

'I'm glad you do. But it wasn't written originally for The Good Old Boys—although it's got Pete and Simon'—these were the Boys' guitarists—'playing on it.'

'Oh, right!'

'Me and my songwriting partner originally saw it as a number that we could submit to Tina Turner.'

'Oh, wow!'

[As surprising as this was, it made sense of those brass inserts, which did not seem to suit the Good Old Boys' style.]

'The demo was put together for that,' Richard went on, 'and Pete and Simon played as session musicians getting a session fee.'

'It would work for The Boys', though,' I said, remembering that powerful riff.

'That's what I thought. When we'd recorded it, it seemed like a good one for the band. The original vocal didn't quite fit, so I recorded another one that took the song in a slightly different direction. But I can't get them to rehearse! That's why I've put them a bit into the background and started to focus on the solo project I told you about.'

'Well, that sounds great—I would love to hear what comes of that!'

He reiterated his promise to do that: 'I'll send you some stuff.'

As we talked, I decided to moot to him an idea that had been working itself to the front of my mind over the previous few weeks.

'I wonder,' I began, 'if you would be prepared to maybe come into school and—you know—do a workshop with some of our Music Technology students?'

He sounded a little cagey.

'What would that involve?' he asked.

'Talking to them about the process of writing a song and demoing it and recording it. Hopefully, you could also do a bit of jamming or something to generate a few ideas—just showing them how it's done really…'

'I wish I could say that there's a formula!'

'But that's exactly the kind of thing you could teach them!'

'I'll have a think. I like to sit and work out ideas with a guitar—I wrote the riff to "Mean Evil Loving Man" that way.'

'That would be perfect!'

'A friend of mine has done a bit of that sort of thing. I'll talk to him and find out what he's done.'

'You'd be great at it! I'll keep in touch and we can come up with some sort of plan for a workshop, if that would be okay?'

He agreed that it could be and we rang off.

Once again, it was Richard's modesty that spoke to me—his modesty about both his song writing ability and his capacity to communicate his ideas to others. On the first count, it seemed to me, he had nothing to prove and, on the second, I couldn't see him being anything other than an engaging and fascinating presenter and group leader.

Whatever was going to happen, though, would have to wait until after the production, which, as these things have a habit of doing, sneaked up on me and began to take over my life. I was fortunate in having a very talented cast, but, even so, choreographing company numbers and coming up with a sufficiently varied and entertaining approach to the script was proving to be a time-consuming affair.

The first night of the run happened to be my birthday and I received two presents: one was a good performance from the cast, the other was a Crosley portable record player from Karen.

The second of these was a novel thing indeed, a retro-styled piece of 3D nostalgia, a time machine. By strange coincidence, I had, only the day before, been reading one of those lifestyle pieces in which some very minor 'celebrity' allows a photographer to wander around her house taking snaps while she witters on about her interior design ideas, the subtext being that she isn't actually doing all that well and most of the stuff on display is consequently pretty cheap and insubstantial.

A link to the article had been posted on Facebook by one of my 'friends' who happened to be one of the 'celebrity's friends and, as you do, I found myself idly glancing at it. Among sundry bits of tat at which the reader was supposed to 'ooh' and 'aah' was one of those very Crosley portable decks. In context, it was clearly being used more for its aesthetic qualities than for any utility it might give, but I was instantly impressed with it as an object, even if I could not know how it sounded from a few photographs.

Opening the box from Karen, I found what looked like a small suitcase with a couple of tiny speakers on the front. Only when open did it reveal itself to be what it was—a music reproduction device. Karen had given it to me because I had, in the previous few weeks, been buying a number of reissues of seven inch singles by the band Iron Maiden. These, such classics (and minor classics) as 'Sanctuary', 'Running Free' and 'Flight of Icarus' had, in their original release form, featured in that collection of rock records that I had divested myself of during my teenage would-be intellectual phase. Now, as a nostalgic middle aged man, I felt enough connection to them to wish to get them back, albeit as facsimiles. The problem had been that I had not owned a turntable for several years. Hence my birthday present.

I placed the thin black disc of 'Running Free' on the deck and lifted the tone arm, an action that began the 45 revs-per-minute spin with all of its promised excitement. Placing the needle into the groove (surprisingly) yielded none of the expected crackle. Instead, the opening drum solo came through crisply.

In truth, the sound from those minute speakers was flat and tinny, but that did not matter. It still had a magical effect on me. That revolving disc became a wormhole, opening up a Star Trek-style rift in time and space, sucking me in and propelling me through an Escheresque tunnel of black vinyl to—where?

Reality corrects itself.

I am standing in a doorway, looking into a bedroom in a modern suburban house. I recognise the place immediately with its carefully arranged line of books, all with unbroken spines, and its art materials and, on the wall, a single poster of Deep Purple Mark II performing live. It's my bedroom, the bedroom I virtually lived in as a teenager. There is a record player on the floor, an original of which the Crosley is a reproduction. Kneeling next to it is a boy of, perhaps, thirteen years old. Actually, I know very well that he is thirteen years old because he's me, younger, thinner and with an admirably full head of hair. He is intent on the record player and is slotting on to his turntable—I think—I strain to see—yes!—he is about to play that original single, the lost single, of 'Running Free'. I half smile as I remember where I bought that: Lotus Records. The drum beat begins….

Does he open the other end of the wormhole in that moment? I can only conclude that he does.

He is suddenly spooked and his head turns in my direction. For an instant, I fear that I am about to be seen—but calm myself when I realise that I would surely remember that having happened. Nevertheless, his gaze is on the space that I occupy and his expression is pensive.

What is he seeing? Is it the future?

Or, is he somehow in empathy with the aching longing that now wracks me, a longing for promise fulfilled or wasted—it doesn't much matter which—and time. Lost, irredeemable time.

I blink. The wormhole closes. I am back in the present. But I feel a renewed sense of connection to the thirteen year old boy I once was.

14—Mandrake Root

IT WAS ALMOST Christmas. The musical had happened and I was kicking about in that slightly exhausted limbo that will be familiar to anyone who has taken part in a challenging, but finite, activity that has now reached, and gone past, its end point. So, for a little relaxation, Tosh, Karen and I went to Birmingham for a gig by another bunch of old rock survivors, Status Quo.

As bands go, of course, Quo have always been characterised by their rather basic approach. Their songs are mostly three chord bashes which never approach the kind of subtleties that a Deep Purple manage. Nevertheless, for us, they were important for two reasons. Firstly, they are unpretentiously and unashamedly entertaining (which was exactly what we needed) and, secondly, they are perhaps the chief exponents of the genre affectionately known to Tosh and myself as 'fuck-off rock 'n' roll'. By this, we mean that it is, in its most fundamental and unadorned sense, no depth, no compromises, like-it-or-lump-it, head-banging heavy music.

The gig did not disappoint. It was everything we could have hoped for: loud, fun and packed with audience participation. It was, indeed, a real tonic, an inspiring blowing away of accumulated cobwebs and it got me thinking about where to go next with the quest or with any projects involving Richard.

It also delighted Karen. In the car on the way back to Nottingham, she was abuzz with good vibes, asking about individual songs and talking about her favourite moments. Afterwards, she confessed that, although she had never really liked heavy rock, she was beginning to come around, citing not only Status Quo, but, obviously, 'Deep Thingy' as bands that she was really starting to enjoy. I sensed that a rare victory for the hardcore fans was in the offing.

I further reflected on the evening with the owner of another of those 'preserved in aspic' record shops. This one was located in my current home town, but, weirdly I had not hitherto visited it despite having lived there for nearly a year.

'They are just a no-nonsense band,' was the owner's succinct and accurate summation of Quo.

Like others of his ilk that I had met on my quest, he belonged to that tribe of old enthusiasts who are following a passion knowing that the pecuniary rewards will never be large. As was typical, his knowledge of the music he sold was encyclopaedic.

'They don't care what people think—they just do what they do,' he went on.

His shop was characteristically small and lined with shelves laden with CDs and music-related DVDs, all packed so tightly together that retrieving any given one of them was anything but a simple operation. There were racks of vinyl records and, perched precariously on high up ledges, a large number of box sets of varying rarity and desirability. The place also smelt disconcertingly of cat piss, although, mercifully, my nostrils quickly acclimatised themselves to that.

I was there for a reason. A friend had been in a few weeks earlier and, browsing its stock, had found five demo CDs of the original 'Concerto for Group and Orchestra' recordings on sale for a very reasonable price. He had promptly texted me a picture and I had made for the place with all convenient speed. Finding the discs in question was the work of moments. They all had plain paper wrappings that simply listed the tracks included. Mostly, these were already publicly available, but one of the discs contained a must-own gem in the form of a commentary by Jon Lord in which he explained what he had been attempting to achieve with the 'Concerto' project. Upon listening to it, the commentary seemed to have been recorded for the DVD release of the filmed concert, but, since that, by then, was nearly impossible to obtain, even from online sources, the discs still seemed worth having: completism again, you see?

'Are these all from the Concerto?' I asked, examining them with a collector's care.

'Yes. They were the sort of thing that was sent out to radio stations and things as demos.'

'Where did you get them from?'

'From a record fair—about ten years ago.'

'Ten years?' I repeated, amazed.

'Yes. I used to have a shop a bit further along the street. Then I spent two and a half years away—in the States, as it happens— then came back and opened up here. I got these while I was running the old place. Just saw them at a fair and snapped them up.'

This insight into the shop owner's background gave me a moment of longing for the bohemian lifestyle that he seemed to have enjoyed. But more practical concerns were at hand: 'Nobody's bought them in ten years?'

He looked a little apologetic: 'Well, people around here don't always know decent music.'

'Do you get a lot of people in?'

'Yes, but this isn't a place for people who like downloads. This is where lovers of real music come—people our sort of age who prefer a more hands-on format. The sort of thing they were used to as kids.'

I wondered to myself what distinction he was making between downloads and real music, but I didn't pursue it.

'I used to have two sets of those,' he nodded towards the demo CDs, 'I sold one to a friend of mine who is the biggest Deep Purple fan in the world.'

'I bet he's not as big a fan as I am,' I said with mock indignation.

'I don't know—he owns everything. He's seen them a few times.'

'So have I!'

'Have you seen the Steve Morse line up, then?'

'Mostly, but I was at the notorious NEC gig in 1993—the one that Ian Gillan said was the worst they ever did.'

'Oh, you mean the one where Blackmore....'

He made the movement of throwing something.

'That's the one. I tell you what—this is how big a Deep Purple fan I am: I booked Nick Simper to do a gig for me. There you go!'

He looked impressed, although, of course, his friend—who, it seems, scoured the country looking for every legitimate or bootleg CD he could find—was really a far bigger Deep Purple completist than I had ever been.

'Nick Simper was in Warhorse, wasn't he?' the owner asked.

'Yes.'

'I saw them play at the Rose and Crown once.'

He gestured vaguely in the direction of a hotel in the centre of town. He went on: 'You know, Deep Purple were supposed to play at the college...' He gave another haphazard nod towards something in the world beyond the stacks and piles of old music—an educational establishment in the suburbs that I knew to be not especially large or, as far as I knew, geared up to host a gig.'—the tickets were printed and everything; I saw one, although I didn't own one. A couple of weeks before the concert, they pulled out. 'Black Night' had just been released as a single and they were committed to going off and promoting it. It was just after Gillan and Glover joined. It was like—we don't do small gigs anymore; we're hitting the big time now.'

'Black Night' had been the band's biggest hit single—at least in the UK. Depending on which chart you believed—there had been several around at the time of its release—it made it to either

Number 1 or 2. Either way, it was the high watermark of Deep Purple's 7" success, although, it must be said that they never saw themselves as primarily a singles band.

The anecdote, though, added to my store of tales about them. On one level, it began to feel as though I was researching and writing a folk history of the band. In other ways, it was another little story that humanised icons, bringing them down to hardcore fan level, filling the gaps in the usual biographies.

I paid the guy, having bargained down the price on the grounds that the CDs had been knocking around for ten years with ne'er a hint of being bought in all that time, and set off for home. The CDs were as interesting and informative as I had hoped they would be. They also got me listening again to all of the Mark I albums.

I lingered over 'Mandrake Root'.

I have already said that it is an anomalously heavy addition to the first album's track listing, but its lyric also bears some consideration. The Mandrake is a plant with a characteristically knotted root that is said to resemble the body of a man—or the devil. According to legend, when the plant is picked, it emits a piercing scream that kills all who hear it.

Perhaps, I thought, there's a metaphor for my quest in that. Remembering the veiled admonishments I had received from the contributors to that Highway Star thread, what I was doing could be seen as plucking a Mandrake—pulling up what should have been left in the ground and producing a noise that should never have been heard.

Equally, though, my actions could have been seen as a positive spin on the legend. Such good old boys as Richard Hudson were Mandrakes of a sort, largely forgotten, left half-buried by time and obscurity; so I was pulling them up and they were producing a sound, but, so what? It was hardly a killer sound and it deserved to be out in public.

Perhaps a Richard Hudson workshop would happen. Perhaps it

wouldn't.

Either way, the acquisition of those demo discs and a chance reading of an interview with Ian Gillan were beginning to draw me back towards the band that had always stood at the heart of this quest, Deep Purple, and the man who had spurred it on in the first place, another Mandrake root with a silent voice: Rod Evans.

15—Shield

BEING A HARDCORE rock fan used to be a lonely life. For a start, your passion of choice is not—and, frankly, never has been—remotely 'cool' (the NWOBHM notwithstanding). In an interview, Roger Glover himself admitted that Deep Purple have at no point been a 'trend', adding, with a hint of irony, that the only fashion that had ever attached itself to the band was one to not like them. As much as Glover inadvertently positioned his own followers as outcasts, it was not without justice. With his greatest love despised, together with a distinctly blue collar 'look', the average heavy rocker has always had trouble fitting readily into a world that favours the whimsical and superficial.

Happily, however, we now live in the interconnected age in which no-one need ever be truly alone and various fora exist for bringing people—even those separated by half a planet—together in the celebration of shared interests.

One such is that bete noir of just about everybody that just about everybody nevertheless uses, Facebook. It is now a rare organisation that has no presence on that platform and bands are no exception. Upon creating my 'wall', I speedily 'liked' the Good Old Boys' page, giving me ready access to all the latest news (there wasn't much of that) and gig information (there was quite a bit of that, though).

As I have said before, I likewise clicked my way on to the distribution list for the Deep Purple page and, for good measure, the Ian Gillan Fan Club, both of which proved to be valuable sources of information about the various doings of the band and its members, past and present.

Many of the posts on the group's page concerned Jon Lord. Indeed, so much of the material that found its way online was to do with concerts that he had done or DVDs and CDs of his music that I frequently had to remind myself that he was no longer with us. Was the internet, I wondered, not only impacting upon the way in which people interact with each other socially, but effecting a change in the nature of death itself? Lord seemed to be enjoying an odd sort of immortality, one from which he could not benefit, it is true, but, in the eyes of the rest of us, immortality all the same. It added an intriguing dimension to the lyric, 'Souls having touched are forever entwined': could the souls of everyone touch via the medium of cyberspace?

This may sound fanciful, especially given that such band pages are public spaces open to all who wish to view them. But a more personal presence in the techno ether came for me courtesy of the Deep Purple Fan Group. This was a somewhat esoteric collective that could not just be joined at will: I submitted a request to be included and was only admitted by the group administrator after what was presumably a vetting process to ensure that my credentials were valid (although how this was done is anyone's guess).

My hope had been that the page would include discussions of songs and albums, filling in the history of the band and yielding some stimulating interpretations of song meanings. I even fancied that someone on there might have some information on the whereabouts of a certain Mr. E. I was to be disappointed on both counts.

While good natured and fun to belong to, the Fan Site consisted largely of members' posted photographs of the band along with YouTube links of performances, interviews and so on. Some of these were valuable: a difficult-to-obtain publicity shot from the early seventies, say, or footage of a concert that had not been released in any other format, not even as an 'official bootleg'. Mostly, though, the links were to often-seen group portraits or studio versions of songs that could be found anywhere. Some were of Deep Purple context bands, such as Rainbow or Whitesnake. The enthusiasm with which they were put online cannot be denied; it was a rare day on which fewer than a dozen links were shared, my Facebook wall rapidly coming to resemble a virtual scrapbook of Purple memorabilia.

More fascinating was the composition of the group's membership. If names are any guide, geography was no barrier to affiliation. Many of the site's members seemed to be located in Eastern Europe; given the band's popularity in that part of the world, this was not surprising. Other names suggested an ardent fan base in the Middle East—and even further afield.

It would be easy to scoff and, it has to be said, there was an artlessness to it all that might have come across as either touching or trite, depending on mood. But it was another manifestation of that love I spoke about earlier and, for that alone, it stood out as meaningful.

It also brought people together. It allowed me, for example, to be wished a happy new year by a woman in Romania who marked the occasion with a YouTube link to Deep Purple's 'Love Conquers All' and then to receive the same message from a woman in Japan (from Tokyo?) with an accompanying picture of every mark of the band.

Both of these site members were a lot younger than the average Deep Purple fan ought to have been, at least on the basis of audience composition at recent gigs I had attended; and they were completely the wrong gender! How could a hardcore Deep Purple fan be a girl?

Not only, then, was the internet taking away the isolation of fanhood (like a sort of geeks' support group), but it was demonstrating that the band's fan base was a lot more diverse than I had previously imagined. While it seemed that, in the UK anyway, their following had distilled down to a hard core of old stagers, elsewhere, it was alive and vibrant and, if anything, growing. It certainly made me realise that my pronouncements on the lot of the hardcore fan may have been more restricted in scope than I had at first thought.

I felt a sense of belonging as part of the Deep Purple Fan Site. It was comforting to know that they were out there, all my fellow devotees, keeping the flame of rock and roll alive. They were not the only ones. Similar Facebook fan sites exist for many rock groups, all checked on, added to and read through with passion and commitment. They are a very tangible manifestation of the hardcore fan worldview and, as such, are to be cherished and celebrated. This, therefore, is my anthem of praise to fan sites, those online conventions or communities of shared sympathy that are fuelled exclusively by the one force that should be behind everything, but is often invisible or diluted beyond recognition— love.

It was on Facebook, too (although not a fan site) that I met, and talked to, perhaps the most significant contributor to my quest, a German musician with a fascinating story to tell.

Before I got that far, though, it was the Deep Purple fan site that made me aware of the next major move in the big wide rock world when someone posted a video of a single taken from the next album by Whitesnake and to say that I was surprised would be an understatement.

The song was 'Stormbringer', the title track of Deep Purple Mark III's second album. Given that David Coverdale had co-written the thing, of course, there was no reason why he should not perform it if he so wished and, indeed, he had been doing so at gigs for some years by that point. What surprised me was the fact that the rest of the album consisted of similar items, re-imagined versions of songs from Marks III and IV, the incarnations of Purple that had featured Coverdale. Its title was even—in a nod to The

Beatles—The Purple Album.

Coverdale's stated motivation was linked in to the passing of Jon Lord. In interviews, he spoke of Deep Purple being his 'university' and of how much he appreciated the opportunity that the 'professors', Lord, Blackmore et al, had given him. Such statements put into perspective his non-attendance at the Sunflower Jam celebration, but also touched on one of the key themes of my own explorations and musings.

Was Coverdale feeling the passing of time? While the album was being trailed, he spoke of how he had reconciled with Blackmore after many years of animosity and of how the two had even discussed the possibility of a joint project (which, it seemed, would have been something like a Deep Purple Mark III reunion). Nothing had come of this, but The Purple Album was a pretty good compromise that seemed to be the work of a man with mortality on his mind and a desire to close accounts. After so many years of forging his own musical identity, this was a facing up to the past and an embracing of it. From a hardcore fan perspective, it was great to see those old songs, moribund for so long, being reclaimed. The version of 'Stormbringer' was excellent: a homage to the original, certainly, but with added oomph and a few modern twists (even if it still left open the question of what a stormbringer actually is).

If I'm honest, though, I was ambivalent about the album in a way that I had not been about Deep Purple's Now What!? I enjoyed it, certainly, but that could not disguise an air of sadness which, for me, surrounded it. I'm not even sure why. Perhaps it was because, for all of its virtuosity and, I believe, sincerity, it was a surrender.

Not to commercialism.

Not to any lack of originality.

But to time.

It was the moment that Coverdale stopped rocking and joined the heritage industry. Whitesnake, the kings of cock rock with a name to match had, in one fell swoop, become a Deep Purple tribute act, with a single original member; in effect, they were no more than a bigger and, probably, better funded, version of Nick Simper's Nasty Habits adventure. They were, for that matter, not so very different from Rod Evans' fake Deep Purple.

It was while thinking about fake Deep Purple—and researching that whole sorry episode—that Evans loomed up large in my vision once more and pulled me back towards my central quest. After months of digressions, the game was back on!

I was put in touch with that German musician I mentioned, a man who knew the people with whom Evans had collaborated on fake Deep Purple and—more excitingly; far, far more excitingly!—claimed to have spoken to Evans himself relatively recently, and not just once, but over a number of years. How I got to know this guy need not be gone into in detail: it is enough to say that someone urged me to contact someone else who had a Facebook friendship with yet another person and so on and so forth.

The upshot was that, after going through what could have been a subplot from a John Le Carre novel, I found myself sitting in front of Facebook Messenger 'interviewing' this faceless, but priceless, source. What I was to discover during a 'conversation' that took up an entire evening would, once again, change my view of Evans, adding more and more mystery to him and his world; as my interlocutor put it: 'there is a lot of shrouded things surrounding all this'.

Not the least 'thing' was his own identity, which, in deference to his nervousness about talking at all, I am placing behind a shield of anonymity, despite his having agreed, under certain circumstances, to be named. In setting up the interview, I felt like Robert Redford or Dustin Hoffman in All the President's Men, meeting a nameless whistleblower in an underground car park (metaphorically speaking) to hear things it was dangerous to know.

It should be said that my source was not particularly interested in Deep Purple (although he offered a passionate defence of fake Deep Purple) being far more concerned about Evans' time with Captain Beyond. Indeed, he said that he had run Captain Beyond's website for a period of time and had even played with several former members of the band (although not Rod Evans): a quick check of his credentials online proved this to be correct on both counts. He was, nevertheless, not entirely comfortable and only reluctantly gave up any secrets at all: many others, I believed, were kept strictly to himself.

It was through his stewardship of the Captain Beyond legacy that he got to know Evans, although, as is inevitably the case with this tale, the process was lengthy and not without considerable complications. It began (he said) in 1998 when he was contacted through the website by a woman named Annie who told him that her husband was a friend of Evans, who he had met at an AA meeting.

Now, of course, I am entering 'tread carefully' territory here; although the implication that Evans has suffered some drink problems has come through from other articles and anecdotes I have read or heard, I am not going to accuse him of being an alcoholic without better proof than that offered by my German friend. The musician felt as much himself, saying that his initial inclination was to view 'Annie' as just another crank feeding him nonsense for her own purposes. He told me, however, that Annie spoke of how she learned of Evans' musical past (I was reminded of my own speculations regarding whether he had ever revealed it to anyone) and had been invited with her husband to Evans' 'humble house' for dinner, an event at which a wall festooned with gold records gave final confirmation of his identity.

At this stage in his life, Evans was not, the musician said, working as a doctor, having hung up his stethoscope sometime around 1996; again, this accorded with other accounts that I had found. Combined with the fact that any Deep Purple royalties that he may have been owed were going straight towards paying off the damages award against him, it seems that this was not a particularly prosperous time for him.

The musician spoke of his scepticism towards Annie and how

he had asked if he could speak to Evans directly. She said that she would ask Evans to send a letter to the musician with an autograph; it should by now be no surprise that no such letter ever arrived, so, convinced that she was at least exaggerating, the musician ended his correspondence with her.

Although the details are a little murky, the next development was that, out of the blue, she re-established a link two years later and finally brokered direct contact between the musician and Rod Evans himself. Quite how and why this came about, I do not know, but she trumped all her previous offers by giving the musician Rod Evans' telephone number.

Rod Evans' telephone number…

I thought about asking for it. Of course I did! But what would have been the point? The answer would have been 'No' and, anyway, as the musician soon revealed, it was no longer active. Another enigma. As he said, 'I could tell you who killed JFK, but Rod is in another league of uncovered mysteries'. As one looking at the mystery from the outside, I had to agree…

The musician was luckier. He told me that he began a telephone correspondence with Evans that lasted from 2003 to 2007, making him easily the person with the most up-to-date information that I have come across (albeit that we are still going back a decade to the final call). From my perspective, a degree of circumspection is required. Like all too many of the glimpses of Evans that I have had, this one is oblique and indirect. I had to take what I was told on trust. Reporting it, then, is a matter for some delicacy and discretion.

On the positive side, the musician, like so many others, described Evans as a 'great person, very smart and eloquent' with whom he had 'great conversations', often lasting for hours. He was at pains to stress Evans' intelligence, telling me that he has an IQ of 160! Perhaps he has: I have already noted that his lyrics bespeak a wide range of reading and, if he did qualify as a doctor, his achievement was one that is rarely matched by halfwits! But the

Evans sketched by the musician was an altogether more troubled soul than I had expected. He certainly did not square with the more breezy character I had pictured from Maria's story or the comments to the Highway Star article or even the figure apparently known to that vinyl-toting Swede. The passage of time may have had something to do with it. I had previously heard about the Evans of the sixties, the eighties, the nineties. This was the Evans of the noughties. They are rare birds indeed upon whom time bestows kindnesses.

The musician revealed that Evans had declined to be involved with Larry Reinhardt's proposed Captain Beyond reunion because he had not been satisfied with the business arrangements. That much could have been guessed. The musician had little—disappointingly little—to say about Deep Purple or fake Deep Purple, saying that he and Evans had not really discussed them because he 'did not wanna open old wounds' [sic].

Several issues vexed me about what I was hearing, or, rather, reading, which were only partly dealt with during the conversation. I was uncertain as to why the musician had broken off the relationship with Evans and he was very clear that it had been his decision to do so. From what I was told, the two had been quite close—to the extent that the musician had offered to arrange a lawyer to fight for the restoration of Evans' share of Deep Purple royalties.

Yet, he told me that he stopped calling Evans.

He said that a meeting between himself and Evans had been set up, but, like 'PN's abortive rendezvous as reported in the comments to the Highway Star article, it had fallen through and there was never any face-to-face conversation. But, given that this had been in 2004 and contact was maintained until 2007, this could hardly have been the reason for the break. There was some reference to animosity between the musician and Evans' wife, who may have suspected his motives in getting in touch, but little detail was given.

'I wonder why I decided to cut loose.' he wrote, musing on his reasons, 'Sometimes it's better to end things on a high note'. In the end, the musician merely said that he was tired of being the one making the effort to keep the relationship alive: I suppose we have all been there.

As my chat with the musician went on, I became increasingly bemused by his failure to bring any of what he had told me out in public prior to that point, if only on a Deep Purple website. His response was interesting: 'Well, why should I? Lots of things I have kept private and always will do so, out of commitment. And the other reason is lots of DP mobsters just bad rep Rod, even to this day, and Rod IS aware of that'.

This led naturally on to the really big question, the one that has been asked less often than might be expected, but the one that cuts to the very heart of my quest: why?

Why did Rod Evans so completely hide himself away?

Other show business figures retire or withdraw from the limelight, but they do not, on the whole, vanish without trace. Ringo Starr, for example, only stopped signing fan memorabilia several decades after the Beatles split and Phil Collins dropped out of the music business for years without ever being totally incommunicado. The musician suggested that, in Evans' case, it was far from an accident, that Evans had deliberately taken steps to ensure that his address and telephone number would be permanently unobtainable. The musician even went so far as to claim that he, himself, was among a select group of five people to whom Evans had opened up, revealing private thoughts and intimate feelings. Still the question remained: why? Why did Evans do it? I pressed the musician on this point.

Again, the response was a little obscure. Words and phrases such as 'scared' and 'almost paranoid' were used. But of what or whom was Evans scared? The chief culprits, as far as the musician was concerned, were the hardcore Deep Purple fan community. Yet, in all my research, I have detected little or no real hostility towards Evans from members of that devoted diaspora.

Curiosity, yes. Apathy and indifference, definitely. But, hostility? No.

Even the fake Deep Purple fiasco does not seem to have been held against him. Besides, as the musician reminded me, 1980 was not strictly speaking the start of Evans' reclusion; he had disappeared from sight in the early seventies when he finally left Captain Beyond. Fake Deep Purple was not a continuation of his music career, but a re-emergence, similar, if less dramatic, than any he might make now. Assuming he has Internet access, Evans could easily check all of this and quickly reassure himself of the general lack of ill-will that people have towards him. Is the answer simply that it is in Evans' character to want privacy and solitude?

I found the conversation with the musician somewhat perturbing, if I'm honest. My quirky little quest had always really been much more about itself than Rod Evans: my chief question had not so much been, 'where is Rod Evans' as 'what makes someone enough of a hardcore fan to want to find Rod Evans'. Now I was thinking more existentially, asking, 'who is Rod Evans?' All at once, he had changed from an abstract, slightly mythical, presence into a complex, problematic individual.

I felt that I was facing the heart of a puzzling darkness in which the mystery of Mr. E had only deepened. I had heard details about him that had not been readily available from any other source, but, if anything, he had become all the more contradictory and paradoxical. My imagination filled itself with multiple Evanses, some ironic, talkative and generous, others brooding, intense and introspective.

There was no way to tell which was the real man, if any, was. All that those of us who took an interest had to go on was his voice, be it on record or at the end of a telephone line. As I ran over what I had learned in my mind, one thing seemed certain: that I would never find Rod Evans. But that did not mean giving up on the quest. The more I thought about it, the more I wondered whether I was doing things the wrong way round: if I could not find him, then, perhaps, there was a way for him to find me. What led me to this revelation was, again, musing about time.

The Deep Purple fan site. The Purple Album. They were backward looking. So, in many ways, was my quest. Rod Evans was gone. He had covered his tracks like some real life Keyser Söze and did not want to be found; my conversation with the musician had convinced me of that. I began to realise that what I had been trying to do was revive the past and the past cannot be revived. The past has gone. The present is forever disappearing. There is only the future.

The projects with which I had hoped to involve Richard at least looked towards the future. When I next heard from him, I learned that the Darwin project recordings had finally got going, although, since they had to be fitted in around other commitments, the time scale looked like being quite lengthy. Nevertheless, one of those promised sneak previews arrived as a very self-effacing email attachment and, frankly, I was knocked flat by it. A gorgeous piano-led piece, it perfectly evoked its exotic and historic subject matter.

I became quite wistful as I listened to it. What a great character Darwin had been! Academic, adventurer, wryly humorous author; he was, to me, the complete package and an inspiration for my own (very much more modest than his!) quest. Richard said the same in relation to his own endeavours.

I don't know how much Richard's new-found enthusiasm for composition had to do with my encouragement. He had a major recording career on his CV, after all. But, somehow, the timing felt right. I had done my bit, however little that was, and a part of the story had come to its end. Okay, so Nick Simper and the other Good Old Boys were not involved and there was not to be, as I had hoped, a new recording of 'Hush', but Richard was in the studio and that pleased me greatly. It seemed like a good time to devote my energies once again to Deep Purple, not to make some forlorn attempt to revive the band's past—I knew that I could not do that—but certainly to celebrate it. Those Facebook pages and fan sites were one way in which it was being celebrated but, if you really want to celebrate the past of rock music, there is only one place to go: the Rock and Roll Hall of Fame.

In essence, the Hall—probably the only famous thing currently to be found in Cleveland, Ohio—is a museum. But, rather than being merely a repository of memorabilia telling the more-or-less objective story of popular music, included artists have to be 'inducted' via a voting process, making it not so much an archive, as an argument, an ongoing debate as to what in the world of popular music is worthy of preservation.

Having a Rock and Roll Hall of Fame exhibit has become a de facto seal of approval or mark of quality. It could be said that, with its ceremonies and citations, entry into the Hall is as close as a rock and roller will ever get to winning a Nobel Prize. It is not surprising, then, that bands and singers have been known to lobby hard to get themselves in and being left out is increasingly seen as a slight or a sign of unimportance and irrelevance.

Deep Purple, somewhat notoriously, spent years being left out, despite all of their contemporaries—many less successful than them—being admitted.

The band that was the highest selling act in America in 1974. The band that has a history stretching back nearly fifty years. The band that—for God's sake!—gave the world 'Smoke on the Water', the riff to which has been banned for being overplayed from more guitar shops than can easily be counted...yes, that band...were not considered good enough for the Rock and Roll Hall of Fame.

They were, according to the nomination committee, a 'one hit wonder' band and, thus, not worthy of induction. Presumably the hit in question is the aforementioned 'Smoke', which, in truth, is probably all that is known of Deep Purple in Cleveland, or, for that matter, anywhere else in Ohio. Even so, it was always a bizarre statement that ignored the many contributions and innovations for which the band has been responsible over the years. In that interview I mentioned in the previous chapter, Ian Gillan sounded pretty resigned about the situation, but I'm not sure that, on his behalf, I was!

My quest, then, evolved once more. Now, my plan was to visit the Rock and Roll Hall of Fame and, hopefully, to suggest to someone working there that it was high time Deep Purple (in all of its marks!) was inducted! I suppose this was when I most saw myself as a questing Knight of the Round Table, although it quickly occurred to me that such an analogy might not have been particularly apt; Don Quixote might have better fitted the occasion. It should be said that the Grail quest comparisons were quite strong, since the trip was conceived and planned in—naturally!—April. Unfortunately, and rather prosaically, there was no time to actually complete it in that most significant of months.

Karen, ever pro-active, got online and found some reviews of the Hall on such sites as Trip Advisor. I read them with interest, but was surprised at how mixed they were. One thing was for certain, though: 'It doesn't sound very perilous,' I said.

Karen looked puzzled.

'Why would you want it perilous?' she asked.

'The quest should end in the Chapel Perilous.'

'What's that?'

I explained that, in various versions of the legend, the Holy Grail is found when a knight, usually Perceval, reaches the rather alarmingly named Chapel, the last resting place of that sacred, but baffling, relic, only to face a number of trials. These are often conceived of as three questions that have to be answered correctly if entry is to be granted.

An analogous story is that of the Fisher King, whose lands are left desolate by a curse, which can only be lifted by a certain stranger turning up and, again, asking a number of questions—usually three—the correct answers to which will restore fertility to the earth. While waiting for the 'one' the king sits by a river, passing the time with an angling rod in his hands; hence the title of the story.

Karen looked at me as though I had taken leave of my senses.

'I thought this was about rock music,' she said, 'not wizards and stuff.'

'Actually, you'd be surprised at how many rock bands sing about wizards and stuff—Uriah Heep, early Rainbow .'

'You're going to a museum, not a chapel, and you're not going to have to answer any daft questions to get in—just pay thirty dollars.'

That, of course, was true, in a strictly literal sense. But this journey felt like it would be about more than the merely literal. Perhaps it would be about the literary. It would certainly be about—by the widest definition of the word—the spiritual.

Karen had another of her brain waves while we were sitting in the cafe of Rough Trade in Nottingham. Primarily a record shop, Rough Trade is the public face of, and retail outlet for, the famous independent label which helped to define much of the sound of the 1980s and which has survived as a home for all sorts of more-or-less creative musicians who would be unlikely to figure too prominently in the latest charts. Although it is a far more ambitious operation than Lotus Records ever was, it is the place that comes closest in atmosphere to that revered crucible of memory and, for that reason, I enjoy going there.

'You should lead a campaign to get Deep Purple into the Hall of whatsit,' Karen said, sipping her hot chocolate.

'The Hall of Fame? What do you mean?'

It transpired that (as I should have guessed) Karen had been quietly researching the whole issue of the band's failure to get into the Hall and had discovered a number of things that I had overlooked. She had, for example, found a link to a Facebook page called 'Induct Deep Purple into the Rock and Roll Hall of Fame'. She had also found some interviews with interested parties in which different reasons for the band's continued exclusion were given, the lamest being that the line-up had changed so many times that it would be difficult to know which mark should be inducted (a similar problem had not prevented Fleetwood Mac, to name just one, being awarded the honour).

Indeed, this was where my greatest hope of a Rod Evans re-emergence lay; on previous occasions when bands had been inducted, there had been impromptu reunions of estranged members, making it at least possible that the man himself might participate.

That this was not an entirely forlorn hope was suggested by my learning, at around this time, that Evans' royalty payments for the three Mark I albums had resumed, meaning that, presumably, the damages award had finally been paid off. Managers and lawyers were, I was told, in contact with him, although, predictably, my information was that he was being very 'elusive' and difficult to get hold of. Even so, I wondered if it all meant that his acceptance back into the Deep Purple family was imminent.

'What do you think I should do?' I asked Karen.

'You could start a petition or something,' she replied.

'I think there have been a few of those already.'

'Yes, but you're really articulate—you could put the case really well. Maybe other people haven't been able to do that.'

I took the compliment, but I doubted that she was correct. After all, the likes of Simon Robinson could hardly have been called tongue-tied and, if people like him had been involved, the case will have been well enough put. Still, there was room for a slightly different approach. I began to give some thought to how the Deep Purple fan site could be mobilised to put pressure on the committee of the Rock and Roll Hall of Fame.

As ever, hovering in the background was the shadowy presence of the mysterious stranger, the long expected guest, Rod Evans.

16—April, Part 2

I HAD DONE precisely nothing when something quite unexpected, but staggeringly serendipitous, happened.

Deep Purple were admitted to the Hall. Nobody thought this turn of events likely. Mere days before the inductees were announced, comments had appeared on the various fan sites and Facebook pages to the effect that this would certainly be another year of disappointment for the band and its fans. It certainly was not. When it was revealed that Deep Purple were to be honoured, there were many expressions of disbelief—more, indeed, than there were of joy or happiness. But, finally, after so much hoping, arguing and lobbying, it was to happen.

I could have seen this as disheartening, but it seemed more like fate playing into my hands. I no longer needed to take any personal role beyond that of witness. And witness I intended to be by, if possible, attending Deep Purple's induction ceremony, which was due to be held in—come on, you've spotted it by now—April. Four other bands were to be let in at the same time—the Steve Miller Band, NWA, Chicago and that Deep Purple support act of old, Cheap Trick—so the event promised to be memorable.

It emerged that the Deep Purple line-ups that were going to be inducted were Marks I-III. All of the musicians included were mentioned individually in the citation, apart, bizarrely, from Nick Simper, whose name was absent, despite his having been a founding member of the band. Exactly what the Hall's nomination committee had against him was unknown and, from an egotistical point of view, his exclusion deprived me of the chance to say that I had once booked a Rock and Roll Hall of Fame inductee to play a gig for me! In an interview published on the Highway Star web site, Simper took his snub philosophically, saying that he would not be 'losing any sleep' over it. More excitingly, Rod Evans, as I had hoped, was among the band members cited: would he be at the ceremony? Would my quest end with some sort of success—or closure, anyway—after all?

In fact, there was, at first, much uncertainty as to which, if any, members of the band would make an appearance. The induction process is essentially a gig, but the elephant in the room was the question of who would play at it: a good word for the history of Deep Purple would be 'tempestuous' and it was far from clear that past and present members would agree to appear together.

Ian Paice was quoted as saying that certain combinations would be literally explosive and would probably end up fighting on stage! If public pronouncements were anything to go by, there was a fair chance that Paice would appear and Glenn Hughes reacted as though all of his birthdays had come at once, but Ian Gillan was positively scathing about the whole affair. He could hardly have been anything else, given the opinions he had expressed about the Hall in various interviews, but he also made the very valid point that to ignore certain members of the current Deep Purple line-up was more than a little unfair.

Steve Morse had been in the band for over twenty years and Don Airey—who had replaced Jon Lord on keyboards—had been around for fourteen years and three albums. It was difficult to see how they were less deserving than some 'older' members who had been in a line up for, maybe, two years.

I could do nothing about any of this, of course, and, besides, my immediate priority was acquiring a ticket for the event. It was not going to be held in Cleveland, but New York, which, in so many ways, was a huge improvement, not least because it would be considerably easier to get to.

Tickets were to be made available at the beginning of February. I learned this by checking the Internet with my iPhone as I sat in a local pub with one of my colleagues. Just along the bar from us was an old guy with close cropped grey hair who nursed a pint of bitter from which he rarely sipped. He objected when we asked the bar man to turn the music down and, only then, did we realise that what we were listening to was a playlist of his jukebox choices. His tastes were diverse. First up was an Ozzy Osborne track, second was a standard by George Formby. The guy was impressed that I recognized a couple of the rockier numbers—my familiarity with the UFO song 'Doctor Doctor' went down particularly well—and the evening then turned into a kind of informal quiz in which he put on tracks which I was expected to name; Led Zeppelin, the Faces and Deep Purple's 'Child in Time' came and went. I was only finally stumped by a Rory Gallagher blues tune.

Perhaps the most interesting thing about our new-found friend, however, was the fact that he claimed to know Ian Gillan. He garbled something about how this had started when the singer had appeared on stage briefly with Ritchie Blackmore's Rainbow, an event that did indeed happen for three nights in the late 1970s.

My colleague and I formed the impression that the old guy had performed with Rainbow and I wondered for a moment if I was in the company of one of the many keyboardists that Blackmore had got through in his endless quest for perfection. No such luck. The guy told us that he played the penny whistle and recorder, neither of which, to my knowledge, had featured with great prominence on any Rainbow song. I began to suspect that I was talking to a fantasist, one who was distracting me from the task of sourcing a ticket for the Rock and Roll Hall of Fame induction ceremony.

The problem was that, it being an American event, the tickets were to be sold only in America and that meant that the chances of getting one in the UK were slim at best. The box office was to open at 9AM on a Friday. I would be at work, even at the real time that they would be made available—2PM UK time. I spoke to Karen and she agreed to access the Internet booking agency on the appointed day to try to get me a ticket.

I entertained next to no hope. With several bands due to be inducted and with so many fans all fighting for the available seats, it was a certainty that they would sell out in minutes. So it proved, at least so it apparently proved. When Karen got on to the Ticketmaster USA website at 2PM and a few seconds, it was already proclaiming that no tickets were left. Fate, it seemed, was dead set against my going to the ceremony to see my quest completed.

But fate had reckoned without Karen.

She called Ticketmaster USA directly and spoke to a female selling agent. The call—from Nottingham to somewhere in the USA—took nearly an hour and so badly prepared was the selling agency for any potential international demand that when Karen was asked to supply a phone number, it had to be an American one; the contact details of a New York hotel that I 'might' be staying at on the night sufficed and Karen prevailed. When I joined her later that evening, she was able to inform me that a ticket would very shortly be on its way.

Fate, quite frankly, never stood a chance.

A confirmation email arrived the next day. That was it! My seat was reserved. The quest would have an ending after all. Okay, I wouldn't be going to the Chapel Perilous, but the venue was the Barclay Center in Brooklyn, so there would be a good chance that peril in some form would not be too far away.

I decided that what I needed to wear on the night was a t-shirt emblazoned with the cover design for The Book of Taliesyn. It was somehow appropriate. I was now seeing myself as a Round Table knight manque and that most Arthurian of Deep Purple related images was the ideal piece of heraldry to sport on any modern day equivalent of a tabard. True, I had never seen such a thing for sale, but that did not deter me. A couple of minutes in the Aladdin's Cave that is the Internet and a t-shirt was ordered and on its way.

I was beginning to feel ready. Ready for the final stage. The completion of the quest—for good or ill.

As the date got nearer, it became clearer which members of the band might be at the ceremony. David Coverdale's Facebook page posted a banner inviting fans to go to see him inducted, providing a link to the Ticketmaster USA web page. It was a good bet, then, that Coverdale at least would be there. It was confirmed that Ritchie Blackmore would not be going, on the slightly odd grounds that he had been banned by Deep Purple's management. That sounded like something of an excuse, but it did increase the potential for Ian Gillan to turn up after all, although loyalty to his current band mates remained a major sticking point.

Eventually, a deal was reached whereby all former members who were at the ceremony would be honoured, but only the then active line-up would perform, the presence of non-inductees Steve Morse and Don Airey notwithstanding. The tantalising possibility of everyone joining together for a version of 'Smoke on the Water' as part of the all-star jam at the end was held out, but there was no guarantee that it would occur. Rod Evans, not surprisingly, remained reclusive and silent. But—who knew?—maybe the impossible—or at any rate highly improbable—would happen and he would emerge from the shadows to accept his award. It seemed too much to dream of, but...but.

Before any of that, my own travel arrangements had to be sorted out. I toyed with the idea of flying to Cleveland and travelling from there to New York, allowing me to take in both the ceremony and the institution that was holding it. That scheme was rejected partly because of cost, but also because it would have involved a fairly excruciating thirteen hour train journey from one city to the other. I knew from past experience that Amtrak is best sampled in small doses and had little yearning to sit cooped up in a gloomy compartment watching the scenery for an entire day, as spectacular as the scenery no doubt would have been. Besides, as Karen pointed out, Deep Purple would not actually be in the Hall at the time of my visit, so it would be largely irrelevant to the quest.

I booked a flight and a hotel in Brooklyn that was a few minutes' walk from the Barclays Center. The night before my flight, Karen and I stayed in a Heathrow Airport hotel. She could accompany me that far, but the final approach to my version of the Chapel Perilous I would have to do alone.

As I sat at a high table in the hotel's bar, I mused on the timing. April, the month of fertility rituals of death and resurrection that had been the basis for Holy Grail stories. What a resurrection it would be if Rod Evans came back from the dead, even if his death had been only metaphorical. I thought also about my own personal quest. It had taken up several years of my life. It was, by now, four years since the passing of Jon Lord, two since the tribute concert in his honour, three since I had got Nick Simper and the other Good Old Boys to play at my mother's birthday party. It had involved much travelling, loads of research, a lot of cold calling and the following of even colder trails.

Yet now an answer was in sight. The story of Deep Purple. The whereabouts of Rod Evans. My own life as a hardcore fan. I knew that the strings of all of those narratives would follow me across the Atlantic and come together at last in the rather blandly named Barclays Center.

The next morning, Karen dropped me at the terminal. After the usual coffee-fueled wait, I climbed the steps of the aeroplane that would take me to New York and the end of the quest.

I am not, I must admit, the best flyer in the world. Predictably, the journey was afflicted with a liberal dose of the clear air turbulence that had provided Ian Gillan with the title for one of the solo albums that he made between stints with Deep Purple. Mind you, I wonder if there is really anyone who does enjoy flying: have you ever experienced a noisy take-off? For the few minutes after the vast metal object all around you somehow gets off the ground, there is invariably an eerie, stony silence as every passenger retreats into a private hell of barely suppressed fear and anxiety. Still, an in-flight movie or two and a couple of alcoholic drinks later, I touched down safely in the USA and was almost there, in New York.

New York. Music. The two seem so well matched. They go together like—well, an old married couple. But, perhaps that's not the right image; it implies autonomy, making of New York and music two different things that just happen to complement each other. I would say that the connection is closer than that: I would say that New York is music. It is surely telling that one of the most arresting representations of the city is the first few minutes of Woody Allen's 'Manhattan' in which a monochrome montage of New York life is presented in symbiotic relation to George Gershwin's 'Rhapsody in Blue'. Paul Morley's eccentric and egotistical (but enjoyable) book Words and Music takes up the theme, tracing the history of pop music using the conceit of it as a modern city.

New York is that modern city. New York is music.

New York has a rhythm track. The thrum of car engines, the judder of subway trains, the swishing high hat of traffic and talk, the percussion of delivery trucks, crowded sidewalks, elevators, clattered plates, hawked newspapers, taxis being hailed, arguments, carnivals, church bells, clocks, aeroplanes flying over, helicopters swooping.

New York has a lead track. Bridges stick out from Manhattan Island like a guitar's machine heads. And the guitar is in the hands of a hard rocker blasting out the chugging riff of a metropolis. But there are solos, too, beginning somewhere around Harlem, jazzy, cool, extempore, until, over Central Park, a more lyrical cadence kicks in, almost folky in its lilt, leading, by a passage operatic in its bombast, through the mansions of mid-town, turning to the screeching, jagged, sweaty wail of Greenwich Village, crashing at last into a cacophony of slides and rumbles at Wall Street.

New York has no voice. No one voice, at least. It has many voices. It has everyone's voice.

New York: busy, varied, chaotic, creative, insane...all words, all a single word for a city that is as much a state of mind as a place.

Summing up New York in a single word, is that the epitome of futile? It would be easy to say so. One word, though, might suffice to convey an individual's reaction to something, anything, so let's give that a go and try to find one.

'Overwhelming'? New York is certainly that, as anyone who has ever emerged from the underground cocoon of Pennsylvania Station to join the human tsunami of Seventh Avenue will know. The length of the streets, the height of the buildings, the sheer noise and bustle...even spending time in any other American city is scant preparation for Manhattan Island. So, how about 'modern'? Again, absolutely. Not for nothing did Fritz Lang base the futuristic setting for his silent classic Metropolis on New York. How many trends have been started in New York or, if not started, reported upon and fostered by the media industry that bases itself there? Music, fashion, art, architecture: New York is, or has been, capital of all of these. 'Unique', then? Yes, although the proliferation of 'NY Lites' across the Middle East and Orient (see Dubai, Hong Kong, Singapore, almost anywhere in China...) have taken away some of that lustre.

If I were going to opt for one word to sum up New York, it would be 'admirable'. Has any other city given itself over quite so completely to gargantuan, beyond-human scale? Pictures of New York from the nineteenth century show it—already a mature city—as a very different place, a place of low rise slums, grimy factories and palaces of the wealthy. This was the city that gave us what is often considered to be the first ever comic strip (the claim is debatable), 'Hogan's Alley', home of Yellow Kid, the original hand-drawn hero. The adventures of the Kid, and a wide ensemble of supporting characters, appeared weekly in a number of New York centred publications and they show the city as a cultural stew made up of economic contrasts, moral complexities and grinding poverty.

Where could New Yorkers go from there, but up? So up they went. Literally. From almost any angle, the city—or Manhattan, at any rate—is defined by the vertical. Vast concrete edifices thrust towards the sky, like the collective fingers of humanity pointing in insatiable demand at God. Grey is the prevailing colour. The grey of stone. The grey of concrete. The shades of grey of countless opinions and beliefs. There is a reason why New York looks at its best when photographed or filmed in black and white (as Woody Allen astutely realised)—it is halfway there already. Grey is its natural palette.

This is not to say that it is ugly. Far from it. This is where it is admirable. When the Hogan's Alleys of old Manhattan began to be knocked down and replaced, it was with something new and never seen before, skyscrapers like the 'Flat Iron Building', so nicknamed because of its shape (New York beat London to that particular trope by a good century). Still a crowd pleaser, it looks rather small and quaint compared to the behemoths that surround it today, but it must have been a revelation when it first appeared. It was among the first of many that subsequently sprang up in New York itself and which have been emulated around the world ever since. London's Shard and Dubai's Burj Khalifa are its great grandchildren.

A lot of those old skyscrapers, the templates that all others have followed, are without question equal aesthetically to the great Medieval cathedrals of Europe or the grand mausolea of Asia. They may sport unpromising names—'The Chrysler Building', 'The Woolworth Building'—but, architecturally, who can deny them the status of masterpieces? Adorned with gothic towers, Art Deco crowns and even gargoyles, they are far more than mere office blocks. They are statements of power. They have their own character, their own shifting populations: city-states-within-a-city-within-a-state.

My first view of that prickly skyline—on this visit as on my first visit years earlier—came from Newark airport in New Jersey, which sits adjacent to New York like a conjoined twin that somehow manages to be drabber, less glamorous and more frumpy than his or her sibling.

The proximity of the two cities touches on something oddly paradoxical about the USA. On the one hand, it is, by any yardstick, the wealthiest and most technologically advanced society the world has ever known. In the last fifty or so years alone, it has gobbled up more of the Earth's resources than the rest of the world combined in all of previous recorded history. It has sent people into space and to the moon and developed weapons that have made it unarguably the world's pre-eminent military power. It has taken computers and other devices to levels that as recently as the 1960s were the fantasies of science fiction writers.

Yet, a traveller's probable first encounter with the USA hardly suggests all of that. On the contrary, the place comes across as a bit folky and down-at-heel. As I emerged from my 'plane in Newark, it was into an airport that, by the standards of Europe or the wealthier parts of Asia, was decidedly lacking in sophistication. The glittering concourses, fashionable shops and high end restaurants that would be found at, say, a Dubai or a Heathrow, were largely absent.

I climbed a couple of staircases and found myself waiting in line to have my passport checked. There was some trepidation attached to this as, on a previous trip to the States, I had arrived at Washington's Dulles Airport to be confronted by a spectacularly rude immigration official. The conversation I had had with him had gone roughly like this:

Official: Purpose of your visit?
Me: I'm a tourist!
Official: Which means WHAT? (There was surely an unspoken 'asshole', at the end of this question)
Me: (Rather taken aback) Well—(thinking quickly) I'm a fan of The West Wing and I wanted to visit some of the places it was

filmed.

Official: The West Wing, huh? So who's the president in that?

Me: Jed Bartlett!

Official: (Denied a bullying opportunity) Oh, right...

On this occasion, however, my visa was issued by an altogether more emollient individual, a young guy sporting a distinctive hipster beard and a welcoming smile. He asked me why I was there and I explained that it was for leisure—specifically, to attend the Hall of Fame Ceremony. To my amazement, when I told him that my main interest was in Deep Purple, he claimed to have never heard of them! Even a mention of 'Smoke on the Water' failed to elicit any recognition; I advised him to get on to Spotify and passed through shaking my head in disbelief.

The journey from the airport to my hotel in Brooklyn can only be described as an odyssey. It began on the relatively plush and high-tech airtrain monorail, but, after a few minutes, I transferred on to a local New Jersey train bound for Pennsylvania Station. Again, I was surprised at how basic and old fashioned this seemed. The seats were high backed benches in two lines along the carriage. They were aged and tatty and, on my side of the aisle (although not the other) they sat three. The free on-train Wi-Fi and buffet cars that would be expected as a minimum in Britain were nowhere to be found. When it got moving, the train shunted and stuttered and farted its way along, passenger comfort not apparently being the chief concern of the driver.

Still, I got to see a bit of New Jersey as we moved at low speed in the direction of Manhattan. What I saw was—well, again, nothing special. Streets of wood slat houses passed by, broken up only by occasional ugly public buildings and areas of garbage-strewn wasteland. It seemed that Americans, in their endless reach upwards, are neglectful of what remains at ground level. Perhaps that sums up America: if you're reaching for the stars, why worry about what you're leaving behind?

Beneath the streets, even less care is lavished. Having reached Penn Station, I transferred to a subway for the last leg of the journey to Brooklyn. New York subway stations, I discovered, are unfussy, to put it mildly. Forget about the elaborate patterns of tiling that you might see in a Paris Metro station or the near cathedral-like architecture that can be found beneath Moscow or those clever double-door things that are common in Hong Kong. New York subway stations are dark and consist of nothing more than a platform and a lot of exposed girders that presumably provide the rather necessary service of ensuring that, say, the Empire State Building does not fall through the ceiling. Clearly, such places are not there to be enjoyed or to be prestigious. They are purely utilitarian: where you get on a train and where you get off it again.

My hotel was just around the corner from the Barclays Center, which has a subway station—a subway station that would have been the ideal place for me to have disembarked. Oh, how I longed to say to a subway employee, 'Pardon me, boy, is that the Barclays Center choo choo?' But I didn't. Instead, I asked the woman in the ticket booth which station would be best for me and she recommended one that proved to be something like a mile from the hotel. Still, the walk gave me my first opportunity to take in Brooklyn. While it was clearly no Manhattan, I certainly did not feel as though I was in a place where my personal safety was under severe threat. I began to relax and even to enjoy myself.

I had two days to spare, so I spent them sightseeing. That part can be got through fairly quickly. Wall Street. Central Park. Empire State Building. Metropolitan Museum of Art. Times Square. Liberty and Ellis Islands. I walked across from Manhattan to Brooklyn. A crowd flowed over Brooklyn Bridge, so many; I had not thought sky-high cab fares had undone so many. I swooshed around as part of the tourist tide. I was surprised at how many French people were visiting the city, but, as I would have predicted, English accents were all around, pretty much all of the time.

My original idea had been to make this a rock and roll themed trip. I was a little late for that. CBGBs, the legendary restaurant and club that had been the spawning ground for a good number of early punk bands, no longer existed and Greenwich Village was only a shadow of the district that had once echoed to the sounds of Bob Dylan on acoustic guitar.

Fortunately, though, Strawberry Fields, the memorial to John Lennon, was still very much a feature of Central Park and a rain-soaked walk along the paths and through the groves of that rectangle of English countryside in the heart of Manhattan brought me to it. At the western edge of the park and opposite the swanky Dakota Building (outside of which Lennon had been coolly murdered that fateful night in December 1980) it is a modest little shrine, consisting of a little landscaping and some floor tiles in a circular design, at the centre of which is a single word, 'Imagine'. While this alludes to Lennon's best-known solo hit, it also poses its visitor a more challenging problem: imagine what might have been had Lennon's life not been cut off at an age that most people would call their prime. Imagine the music, the activism, the craziness. Imagine the art, the art that he produced, the art that he lived, and imagine what you could be, what the world could be. To me, that simple, tasteful mosaic by the side of a busy road was another reminder of how rock music and time are constantly at odds with each other, the one demanding limitless horizons, the other forcing us all down an ever-narrowing track.

I was thinking about Strawberry Fields on the evening of the defiant subjugation of time that was the Induction Ceremony. I showered and put on my uniform of leather jacket and that precious 'Taliesyn' t-shirt. The effect, it must be admitted, was ruined somewhat by my being forced, due to the chilly weather, to wear a jumper over the all important album cover motif, but, hey, I knew that it was there, even if no-one else did.

I stepped into the hotel lift. A guy, perhaps a little older than me and wearing a cold-busting hoodie, was already in there. I nodded to him with perfunctory politeness before noticing that his t-shirt was partly exposed, revealing, in Gothic script, part of a phrase: 'ep Pur'.

'Is that,' I asked him, 'a Deep Purple t-shirt?'

'Yes!' He replied in some surprise, adding, 'Do you like them, too?'

I lifted up my jumper to reveal the design on my own chest. He laughed. The ice broken, I pressed him further: 'So, are you going to the Rock and Roll Hall of Fame Induction Ceremony?'

'I am,' he said, 'I only decided to go at the last minute. Should be good, though.'

I found his words a little strange. If the event had sold out quickly, how could he have obtained a ticket so late in the day?

The short walk to the venue was along Third Avenue and the evening was reasonably pleasant, the low temperature notwithstanding. One thing I had rapidly discovered was that a Brooklyn avenue is not remotely like its Manhattan equivalent. I passed none of the skyscrapers, plush boutiques and gridlocked traffic one might find on Woody Allen's favourite island. Brooklyn's Third Avenue was actually rather quiet. The tallest buildings were a couple of social housing projects that made it to around seven or eight stories. Apart from those, there were a few scuzzy-looking delis, a drab bodega and two petrol stations that, again, made few concessions to customer convenience.

Turning the corner, however, revealed the Barclays Center, which was undeniably impressive. A monumental curvy tortoise of brown tiling and glass, it rose from its unprepossessing surroundings like a movie monster waking from slumber. At its front was a plaza over which hung a vast concrete circle, like a crown, into which was built a video screen showing ever-changing adverts and promos; it looked like it could not possibly stay up there, but somehow it did. On its outside edge the sponsor's logo was displayed in letters that, themselves, must have been of gigantic proportions. I was struck by how strange it was that those letters spelled out the name of a British bank with almost no visible presence in the USA. After all, no one would expect a Premiership football ground to be called (say) The Chase Manhattan Stadium.

Although I had allowed myself a generous hour before the given start time to get there, a crowd had already assembled and I joined a queue at a considerable distance from the Center itself. In front of me was one of those old guys that are only possible in the USA, a blue collar type with a short grey beard, an ear ring, a leather jacket, shades and (finishing touch) a bandana over his head. He was the type who somehow manages an air of rugged cool despite, or because of, advancing years. His t-shirt summed him up very well, being black with the boast 'I may be old, but that means I got to see all the cool bands live' screaming from it in stark white letters. He had his (by the looks of it, twenty-something) daughter with him and they were speculating on which members of which bands would be there.

'Who are you here to see?' I asked, butting in to their conversation.

'All of them, man,' the old guy said, 'I just like music. I like 'em all. Who are you here for?'

I explained that Deep Purple were the band that had drawn me there, but that I also liked most of the others.

'You're from England,' the man's daughter correctly deduced.

'It's the accent, isn't it?' I said, 'It's a bit of a giveaway…'

'Have you come from England just for this?' She went on.

The simple answer—the one I gave her—was 'yes', but there was so much more to it than that….

'You must be quite a fan,' she said.

Actually, I thought, I'm quite a hardcore fan…

The queue began to shuffle forward. Once through the glass doors, we were all subjected to a security check of a thoroughness that would have been the envy of many an airport. My clearance obtained, I entered the cavernous lobby space.

It was only then that I began to notice the makeup of the crowd around me. There were far more Cheap Trick t-shirts than I would have expected. The average age of my fellow attendees, however, was no surprise. Most were at least of my vintage, but, then, the bands that were to appear had all been around for decades, so these people were like me—they had grown up with their heroes and were there to see them duly honoured. I bought myself a beer (for an amount that I initially took to be a joke and which certainly ruled out any possibility of my getting drunk) and went in search of my seat.

I found it high up and to the left of the stage. It gave me a pretty good, if long distance, view of proceedings. The stage was for the most part unadorned: a few video screens towards its rear and above and around it were about all the set in evidence. The whole thing, though, was framed by a vast neon arch that glowed blue at first, but which would go on to change colour and pattern to suit whichever performance was happening on stage at any given moment. In front of the stage and extending into the auditorium were round tables, set out as for some polite gala luncheon. This was where the bands, their guests and others associated with the ceremony would be seated. I wondered how weird it would be to be sitting at a table, sipping a drink, knowing that several thousand people were watching from the surrounding shadows.

I sat down next to a young guy, who immediately struck up a conversation. Like me, he was there for Deep Purple, about whom he spoke in an authoritative tone, despite getting almost every fact about them wrong. He was most keen to see if Blackmore would turn up; when I told him that I was hoping that Rod Evans would appear, he was totally befuddled, having no idea who I was talking about.

'He was the singer with the Mark I line-up,' I told him.

'Wasn't that Gillan?'

'That was Mark II.'

'Oh…' He went quiet for a moment, before adding: 'I thought Coverdale was Mark II.'

'That was Mark III.'

He appeared a bit confused.

'I like the Coverdale version of the band.'

'And Glenn Hughes,' I reminded him, 'and so do I—they produced three great albums.'

Now we seemed to be on more solid ground.

'I really want them to play 'Burn',' he said, enthusiastically.

I felt a little mean in puncturing his illusions:

'Given the line up that will be performing, that's not going to happen,' I said.

'Coverdale's here.'

'He's not going to be performing.'

Facts did not get in the way of this guy's excitability.

'I really wanna hear 'Burn'!' he repeated.

The audience grew as the start time got closer, but the arena did not completely fill up. From my vantage point, I could see quite a few empty seats: not huge numbers, it is true, but some, and that, in itself, was not what I had anticipated. I mentioned this to my new found, short term friend.

'It's not sold out,' he told me.

This chimed with what the guy in the lift had said about only deciding to come at the last minute. Of course, it did not make Karen's achievement in acquiring a ticket from England any the less impressive, but it did suggest that my panic-stricken urgency about the whole matter had not been entirely justified.

The tables in the area in front of the stage were by now occupied with some pretty famous people and the ceremony finally got going. It was quite a slick affair, on the whole. There was no compère as such: things just sort of happened, but that was fine—it all worked well and had clearly been meticulously rehearsed. The whole event, despite being very long (over four hours), moved along at quite a tempo.

David Byrne, erstwhile lead singer of Talking Heads, came on to perform a David Bowie song as a tribute to that recently departed rock giant. It was a classy way to begin and reminded me of what a great performer Byrne was and what a superb songwriter Bowie had been. Of the former, I mentally resolved to get myself a ticket if, and when, he toured again. There were a couple of other such moments during the evening: Sheryl Crow gave us a song and there was an 'In Memorium' section, which, strangely, included as many record company executives as artists.

Each of the bands to be honoured was introduced by a short video montage of images and sound clips that roughly sketched their careers, before being formally 'inducted' by a different, although genre appropriate, rock musician. A couple of members of The Black Keys, for example, inducted Steve Miller, while Kid Rock did the same for Cheap Trick. The induction took the form of a fawning speech that was answered, at considerable length, by the inducted bands (and, in the case of Steve Miller, in so controversial a way that Dan Auerbach of The Black Keys later expressed regret at having taken part). Speeches over, each band got to play precisely three of their songs, unless that is, they were NWA, who talked for ages and then left the stage without sharing so much as a note.

NWA member Ice Cube did, however, strike one important chord (pun intended) with me. Responding to criticisms that, as hip hop pioneers, the group was not strictly speaking 'rock and roll', he questioned what is meant by that much used term. It is, he said, not an instrument or even a style of music, but an attitude, or, as he put it, a spirit. To him, it was a spirit of individuality, innovation and defiance of convention; the musical style did not even matter. I could only agree.

But, the first inductees to be given their award were none other than Deep Purple. Lars Ulrich, drummer with the heavy metal (and, therefore, Deep Purple influenced) band Metallica, performed the induction. He spoke of how Deep Purple had helped to define a genre and should always be spoken of in the same breath as Black Sabbath and Led Zeppelin, both of whom had long since been inducted. He spoke, memorably, of the band's 'legacy without end' of great songs. He offered mild criticism of the Hall for not letting them in sooner, accounting for it by suggesting that their massive international following was not matched in the United States, where they were something of an unknown quantity. He praised the individual members, drawing a particularly loud cheer for the absent 'Ritchie fucking Blackmore' and then…

Then, he said something that made my heart stop and had me sitting upright in my chair…

Ian Gillan, Ian Paice and Roger Glover were present—that was known. But, then Ulrich mentioned 'the three other inductees here tonight', David Coverdale, Glenn Hughes and 'last, but actually first'—Rod Evans, 'who was the voice of the formative Purple in the late 1960s and on their first single "Hush".' He then added, 'Don't be shy.'

The three other inductees here…here!

That was what I had just heard, wasn't it? Was Rod Evans in the room? Was he sitting at one of those tables no more than twenty or thirty metres away from me?

The mystery was not cleared up when the band went to respond and to receive their award. Gillan, Glover and Paice were present, as was Jon Lord's widow, Vicky. Coverdale and Hughes were there, too. But there was no Rod Evans. That, of course, did not mean that he was not in the hall: could that 'don't be shy' have been an exhortation to go up on stage with the others? And Ulrich had said 'here', hadn't he? Hadn't he?

Well, maybe not.

According to a transcript of his speech that appeared on the Rolling Stone website the following day, he had said, 'the three other inductees tonight'; there was no 'here', despite my having been convinced that I had heard it. And 'don't be shy' could have been a general call for Evans to get back in touch with the fans rather than a practical invitation to someone near at hand. In fact, there was no further mention of Evans' name either at the event or in later reports, which there surely would have been—on some Deep Purple fan Facebook page if nowhere else—had he chosen that night to end his thirty six year silence. His absence was confirmed by various websites in the ensuing days.

So, I had made it to the Chapel Perilous—or the Barclays Center, at any rate—but, just as the Holy Grail seemed within my grasp…I realised that it was not there after all.

Or was it?

The band members made their speeches, which were conventional catalogues of 'thank yous', albeit laced with generous tributes to Jon Lord, and then the current line-up got on with the three songs. Their opener was a solid 'Highway Star' (the young guy next to me criticised Steve Morse for 'missing notes' during the guitar solo, even stating that he could have done better himself; I silently mouthed a 'yeah, right' as he spoke).

Next was a brief medley of 'Green Onions'—in honour, apparently, of Jon Lord—and one of the songs that American audiences might recognise, 'Hush'; how sweet it would have been had it been essayed by its original singer. The set concluded with— well, what do you think? Everyone knew that one. The second the opening notes of that thundering, immortal riff sounded—DA DA DA—the audience went wild. But the promise that Hughes and Coverdale might come out on stage for a general jam was, sadly, not met. It did seem like the latest in a long line of missed opportunities.

I had heard those songs so many times before in so many different arrangements, but they still thrilled me. I sat, open mouthed, grabbed, shaken, pulled into the electronic cadences and throbbing rhythms, and, for a moment, the arena faded around me. I sat there, looking into the heart of light, the silence.

Words and sounds jumbled in my imagination. A shadow passed across the vast space.

What could I do but chase it?

Adrian Jarvis

17—April, Part 3

CHASING SHADOWS, OVER my walls, with myself hardly sleeping. All I'm asking some secret voice is to lead me to darkness. There's a black hill I have to climb. Satan's world? It's all done by feel, past castles white and fair, past dreaming chessmen on their boards, with a fool's mate as a snare. I'm losing time and my mind. Well, here's my views, I always lose—things I want to do are yesterday's news...if only I could see you, to see if you are laughing or crying.

The arena is gone. Where am I now?

Am I still in Brooklyn or is this the garden of earthly delights? Is there even a difference between the two? Perhaps it's the intricate ink lines of John Vernon Lord's Book of Taliesyn cover. Whichever, I seem to be a bit lost.

But, help is at hand, it seems. There's a dot in the (purple) sky. It's coming towards me, travelling at huge speed. It begins to assume a shape of sorts. There's something flapping around it. As it comes ever closer, I see that it's a cape and it surrounds a person. Then that person becomes a man. He's wearing a tight-fitting lycra costume. Is he—no, it can't be!—a superhero? Superheroes only exist in those comics I've secretly never stopped reading, don't they? But, yes, as he comes in to land elegantly in front of me, I see that he is indeed a superhero. A rather old one, it must be said, with spindly arms and the suggestion of a gut. He's wearing a costume that is a deep shade of purple and on his chest he has a large

"B" rendered in a curly sixties-style font. A mask covers half his face, but there is definitely something familiar about that chin.

'Who are you?' I ask, still somewhat bemused by both him and my surroundings.

'Take me as I am,' he begins, 'an excuse for a man.'

'What?' I ask.

Then I realise. That's a Mark I lyric. And that description of my journey here that you'll find back there somewhere—they were Mark I lyrics, too. I think I'm beginning to get a handle on where I might be.

'Who are you really?' I press him.

'Maybe once in a while I'll forget and I'll smile—' he says.

'Enough with the lyrics!' I say.

'All right,' he says, 'I'm here to rescue you. I am Captain Beyond!'

I'm not fooled by that.

'Mmm", I reply, "You look distinctly like Rod Evans to me.'

He is angered. Whatever superpowers he possesses threaten to overwhelm him. He raises his arms to the sky. I am expecting a thunderbolt, but all I get is words.

'That name is lost!' Captain Beyond intones in a deep, slightly croony, voice.

'No it isn't!' I say, 'I've been looking for its owner.'

Calming down, he asks: 'Have you found him?'

And I am forced to admit, with a shamed downward glance: 'No.'

'I—he—never wanted to be found,' he says.

'You've given yourself away,' I tell him, 'You are Rod Evans, aren't you?'

Captain Beyond rubs his chin for a long time. Finally, he says: 'Clearly, I'm not really Rod Evans because this is your dream or reverie—or, maybe, it's a metaphor—whatever: it is not a real place. Therefore, I cannot really be Rod Evans. But, the more interesting question is—who is Rod Evans anyway?'

I remember my conversation with the musician and how it made me ask that very question. The answer still seems frustratingly distant.

I sigh.

'That's what I've been trying to find out,' I say in some exasperation.

'No. You're missing my point,' he says, 'What I mean to ask is: what does Rod Evans represent?'

'He's a rock singer who went AWOL,' I say prosaically.

'In a literal sense, yes,' he replies, 'But is that all he is?'

I decide that I might as well engage with this philosophical fantasy figure and say: 'On a lot of levels, yes. He has fans all over the world who are desperate to find out something about him—and he turns his back on them. In fact, why am I using the third person? You! You have turned your back on all your fans!'

He looks a bit hurt and I regret the severity of my words.

'I'm entitled to wear this mask if I want to,' he says, 'Why shouldn't I have a private life? Other people do.'

The contributors to that Highway Star thread would have agreed.

'But the fans…' I flounder helplessly, 'They want to hear from you.'

'They have heard from me,' he says, 'Don't you think that my silence communicates a very eloquent message?'

I have to admit that he's right. He presses home his advantage: 'I spent some time in the public eye and, at that point, I was happy to be available to whoever wanted my attention; you've read the interviews. But I decided to leave that behind. I have that right.'

'Yes,' I say, 'but there is so much we can learn from you…'

He laughs and time-lapse clouds charge through the surreal sky.

'Like what? How I came up with the lyrics to "Mandrake Root"? It's hardly deep wisdom.'

'But you are loved by so many people.'

'I didn't feel much love in 1980,' he tells me with a melancholic undertone.

He is right, of course. The fans had their chance. Fake Deep Purple was always going to be a shambles, but things didn't have to turn out that way. There were other directions in which Rod Evans could have gone if he had received sufficient encouragement. But Mark I never gained the traction among fans enjoyed by Marks II and III. We can't complain.

'So my quest has been a failure,' I state baldly.

'No,' he says emphatically, 'I return to my question: what does Rod Evans represent?'

Now I know what he means. Now I understand the persona under which he is presenting himself; he is here to make me see beyond simple, straightforward answers. He's right. What I have been trying to find out is not where Rod Evans is, but what he stands for, what he symbolises. To me.

'Can I quote one more lyric?' he asks.

I nod my assent. He speaks: 'Three times I have been born; I know this from meditation.'

I recognise this from the Book of Taliesyn track 'Listen, Learn, Read On', but I frown, confused as to its relevance. He glosses for me: 'The first time I was born was as the singer with Deep Purple. The second time in my medical career afterwards. The third time as a recluse.'

He's prompted a question—as he intended to: what have been my three births? I shake my head. I don't know.

'Come on,' he says, 'Let me show you something.'

He unfurls his cape. It is long, long enough to cover his whole body like a silk purple shroud. I take the end of it in my hands and, suddenly, we are airborne. He is ahead of me, powering us towards the sky. I am bumping along behind, hanging on to the cape for dear life, buffeted by the winds. At first, I feel terror, then, as I get more comfortable, apprehension, until, composed at last, I begin to enjoy myself. I look at the rushing ground below me. The orgiastic twistings and dematerialisations of Bosch's masterpiece give way to the no less weird, but more stylised, drawings of John Vernon Lord. Then, the view changes again, in unexpected ways.

I see myself as a teenager in Lotus Records, delicately holding that vinyl copy of the third album, my eyes moving over the gothic artwork of its cover in wonderment. I see myself in my bedroom later, putting the record onto that old turntable with the tiny, tinny speakers; the sound quality is terrible, but the music is unmistakeable. There's a smile on my face.

Then I'm at school, talking with my friends about Deep Purple. There's Paul! I attempt a wave, but it's hard while clinging to Captain Beyond's cape and Paul wouldn't be able to see me anyway. Paul and I seem to be the only ones who are interested in the band. Everyone around us is into Duran Duran, Haircut 100 and Culture Club. Even from up here, I can see that the teenage me is resolving secretly to not follow the crowd, to stick to what he believes in and to like what he likes. That's my first birth.

Now we're over Oxford. It's even more beautiful from up here than it is from the ground. The dome of the Radcliffe Camera, the towers of All Souls, Tom Quad—they all shine in the sunlight as though illuminated with an inner glow. There I am, walking awkwardly through my college, Keble, with some cassettes in my hand. I can see that one of them is the Mark III album, Stormbringer which I've just bought from someone for a token sum.

I'm not dressed like most people around me. I would call it individualistic, but there's no getting around the fact that I am just plain scruffy. So, I've taken that 'not following the crowd' thing to heart, then! I see myself in tutorials, causing bemusement to both my fellow students and my tutors with some of my more outlandish ideas and there I am when it's all over, sitting in the Sheldonian Theatre, waiting to graduate. I'm wearing the academic uniform known as "subfusc" this time, so I blend more easily into the general picture. I do know that I have not got a job lined up and no intention of going along the conventional route of looking for one in the City or in the media; that individualism again! But, I would rather follow my heart than a big pay packet. That's my second birth.

We're back over the West Midlands. There am I with my ex-wife. She's something of an individualist herself and she definitely does not like Deep Purple. But, I still get her to go along to a couple of gigs. There we are at the NEC in 1998. I lean over and give her an appreciative hug when she correctly identifies the opening song as 'Ted the Mechanic' from Purpendicular. There we are again at the Royal Albert Hall in 1999 for the 'Concerto for Group and Orchestra' revival.

We end up arguing that night. I see now that we are doing a lot of arguing at this point in our relationship. It makes me sad.

Captain Beyond and I are over a different landscape now. My ex-wife is gone. There are other women, but nothing that lasts. I see myself occupied by various projects—gaining a black belt in taekwondo, studying for a masters degree followed by a doctorate. I would call them the achieving of goals, but they could as easily be seen as passing time and filling in gaps. Still, there I am at my PhD graduation having my picture taken by one of those disposable 'friends' you meet at such occasions. I'm standing next to Karen. Captain Beyond and I begin to descend.

We land in the hazy borderland between reverie and reality. I can hear the music and voices of the induction ceremony drawing me back to the world; there isn't much time.

'What was my third birth?' I ask, hastily.

'I don't know,' he replies, 'Maybe it hasn't happened yet.'

His cape is flapping. A wind is blowing and I know that he means to ride it.

'Don't leave,' I say.

Even through the mask, I can see that his expression is one of disappointment.

'If you say that to me, then our journey has been for nothing,' he says.

I know that my words were badly chosen.

'It hasn't been,' I reassure him.

He smiles.

'You never left, did you?' I say.

'No,' he confirms, 'I've always been there. In the music and in what it means to you.'

'If I need you, I won't need a bat signal, will I?'

'No. Just stick the record on the turntable, put the needle in the groove and—what?'

He can see my look of sceptical indulgence.

'Actually,' I say, 'I'll just put it on my iPod if it's all the same to you.'

'Yeah, okay, that'll work, too,' he says, 'and so will this: listening to Deep Purple as they ascend to the pantheon of the greats.'

By now the distinctive notes of live rock 'n' roll are filling my ears and my consciousness.

So we shake hands and Captain Beyond mounts the air. In a few seconds, he has contracted into that dot in the distance and, in a few seconds more; he has disappeared altogether into the cloud-strewn purple sky. Then the sky itself melts away, cross-fading into the arena and the music.

There's not much more to say. It occurred to me as I sat high up in that audience how often I had managed to be present at significant moments for Deep Purple, or the most recent marks of Deep Purple, at least. I had been at the notorious 1993 NEC gig, I had been at the revival of the 'Concerto for Group and Orchestra', I had been at the Albert Hall to celebrate the life and music of Jon Lord. Here I was again, watching the band enter the Rock and Roll Hall of Fame. Although not part of the same sequence, Blackmore's Rainbow gig at the NEC fits in here, too. The life of a hardcore fan....

Deep Purple would go on into the future, but that night in Brooklyn seemed like an ending; not a terminal ending, to be sure, but perhaps the ending of a phase.

Somehow, it brought everything together, giving me a conclusion—not, I admit, a conclusion to the quest in its most simple sense, since Rod Evans is still out there somewhere, lost in time.

You never know, he might read this and get in touch.

Perhaps, then, the end of the quest is yet to happen. Perhaps that would be my third birth. If I am honest, though, I am not all that hopeful. If the induction ceremony was not enough to get Rod Evans to reveal himself, the ramblings and musings of an old fan are not likely to have much impact. Still, I had a different sort of conclusion. If I had not found Rod Evans, I had found Nick Simper (of whom I was a fan in spite of his constant omission from reunion guest lists), Alan Barratt and the rest of The Good Old Boys: all lovely guys and superb musicians. I had found Ian Hansford, Mick Angus, Maria from Milan and the anonymous German musician. I had also, of course, found Richard Hudson, a gentleman and true creative soul. Somehow, I had got the right cryptic crossword answer, but without really working out the clue; as any cruciverbalist will tell you, that sometimes happens and the answer is no less satisfying for it.

Just as significantly, I had explored in depth what the music means to me and how it is one of the key elements that add up to who I am. On a not unrelated point, I had discovered the connection between music and friendship, the way music helps to forge a bond. Finally, I had realized that this quest had actually been a disguised love story and not, as I am sure you are expecting, between myself and the music or between myself and Deep Purple. It had been a love story between myself and the woman who had encouraged my search, who had been there for much of it, who had, indeed, facilitated many of its key stages. Karen.

As I have suggested several times, the cover to The Book of Taliesyn is an intricate puzzle. The artist seems to have intended this: on its extreme right is a disembodied lock, a lock without a key. The whole image is crowded with ink lines and pathways and circles, none of which go anywhere but all of which mesmerise like some primitive 'magic eye' picture; yet, for all that, it does have some sort of meaning. At various places in the bizarre composition can be seen musicians, or, rather, minstrels, since they are dressed in medieval clothes and play medieval instruments. I have always assumed that they are meant to represent the members of the band. The style of the drawing is such, however, that identifying specific individuals is impossible.

But that, in itself, is the meaning. Presumably, one of those flat, mono-tinted figures is supposed to be Rod Evans, but which one? Who can tell, and, after the journey I have taken, what does it matter anyway?

Postscript: Shadows

THE BOOK HAD been out for about a fortnight and I was on my way down for a weekend at Loz's holiday cottage in the county of Somerset. I had just pulled in to a service station to refuel when my phone rang. I could see from the display that it was Richard Hudson. His timing was good: a minute or two earlier and I would have been on the road and not able to answer. But, then, Richard is a drummer—good timing is what he does.

'I just wanted to say that I've read your book,' he said.

'Did you enjoy it?' I asked.

'Loved it! I stayed up all night reading it—I couldn't put it down!'

This was exactly the reaction for which I had hoped. He went on: 'I just wanted to say thank you for all the kind words.'

'They were no more than the truth.' I said, 'I'm really pleased that you like it!'

'I do! Pity you didn't find him.'

'Oh, well! Maybe he'll turn up.'

'Yes. But the book isn't really about that, is it? It seems to me that it's about a lot more than that.'

I appreciated his praise and told him that he was a perceptive critic: the book is about more than that. We chatted for a while longer and hung up with the usual undertakings to get together at some point for a drink.

I include this brief anecdote not as a sop to my ego, but simply because I can. Time has moved on. The last of the incidents described in the foregoing narrative occurred nearly two years ago and the UK version of the book has been available (in the UK) for half that time. I now sit in Malaysia preparing the U.S. edition (don't ask what I'm doing in Malaysia—that tale will be told soon enough...) and have a good opportunity to build on what I already have by considering where the story is now, because it will be somewhere: time never stops and no story is ever completed, only abandoned.

Gratifyingly, Richard's feedback was not untypical. I received a lot of personal communications from people who had read the book and felt that it spoke to them. Then there were the comments concerning the whereabouts of Mr. E himself.

If, though, you are hoping that this coda is about to report the successful end of the search for Rod Evans—well, there's no easy way to let you down...he's still out there. Some of the people who contacted me stated that Ian Paice knows exactly where Evans is currently living, despite, in interviews, his always having categorically denied this. Others said that they knew for a fact that Evans was living under a pseudonym in California.

On closer examination, this proved to be another red herring: no-one knew the pseudonym and, anyway, it might not be California, it might be Maine, or so one of their friends said, who heard it from another friend who met someone who—and so on.... For a week or two, a photograph of an aged Rod Evans found its way on to various Deep Purple related Facebook pages; this generated a modicum of excitement until it emerged that it did not depict Rod Evans, the erstwhile rock singer, but Rod Evans, the lawyer from Eastbourne on the South Coast of England.

Someone else directed me to a site on which an American woman who claimed to be a personal friend of Evans had posted a photograph supposedly showing her and her family on a day out with him. Unfortunately, not only was the picture years out of date, but whoever the guy in it was, he could not have looked less like Rod Evans if he had been wearing Quasimodo prosthetics.

Most promisingly, Maria from Milan told me via Facebook Messenger that she had tracked down Evans' children on social media, but was unsure what to do about it. She claimed to have discovered that Evans had intended to go to the Rock and Roll Hall of Fame induction ceremony, accompanied by his son, but, for whatever reason, pulled out at the last minute. It was an intriguing nugget of information that made me realize how tantalizingly close the quest had been to a successful outcome, but, in itself, it was another dead end. By her own admission, it got Maria no closer to uncovering Evans' whereabouts; if his children know where he is, they are not talking.

The anonymous German musician also got in touch to inform me that he was trying to affect a fake Deep Purple reunion. While such a thing would have considerable novelty value, it is difficult to see Evans showing up to the party: it is to be imagined that he is not overly nostalgic about that period of his life.

To my mind, all of this activity begged a crucial question. A small number of Internet forum posts took the line of 'if Rod Evans does not want to be found, who is this Jarvis guy to go poking around looking for him?' You who have read this far will know that I was very conscious of this issue and that I was assiduous in avoiding the invasion of anyone's privacy when conducting my research. But, in some respects, I do not disagree with those username-anonymized posters in that I have, quite frequently, asked myself whether finding Rod Evans is something I really want to accomplish. Or, rather, I have wondered what purpose his finding would serve.

What would he actually be able to tell us?

Yes, he could solve the mystery of what he has been doing for nearly forty years, although, given that it would almost certainly amount to no more than an average career in some aspect of medical care, his revelations would supply a thrifty paragraph at most. More interestingly—perhaps pricelessly—he could speak of his feelings about everything that happened: this would be especially valuable in the case of the fake Deep Purple debacle.

But that is about all. The truth is that what you have read is probably as full a biography as Rod Evans needs or, frankly, deserves. As cruel as it may sound to say it, his disappearance is by far the most interesting thing about him. Everything else is relatively commonplace. It is best to leave him, then, shrouded by shadows, a figure of fable and legend, a King Arthur who left the field of battle wounded, making a promise to return, a promise that, as the years pass, looks less and less likely to be kept.

And, really, isn't that the best service that he can render us? Some of those people who got in touch after reading the book told me that it had moved them; one candidly said that he reached the end with 'tears in his eyes'. Yet, the story is not particularly tragic or sad: the ending, indeed, is rather triumphant. But, as much as it recounts a moment when Deep Purple were at one of their peaks, the real triumph is that of the fans. The quest was not about finding Rod Evans so much as sharing experiences and feelings that we—the fans—have all had and which touch profoundly on who we are as individuals.

Ultimately, that is what a band is.

Its members are important, of course, but they are only one side of an unbalanced equation. When we speak about 'Deep Purple', we are referring to Gillan, Glover, Paice and everyone else who has stood on that stage with them, but, more so, much more so, we mean the thousands upon thousands of people all around the world for whom the music is a living soundtrack to loves and fears and hopes and dreams. I like to think that Rod Evans knows this: that a lost prophet in a wilderness of speculation can fire the imagination in ways that an old man with a few memories, and not much else, never could. Rod Evans the Myth is a catalyst to our lives; Rod Evans the Man could only ever be a disappointment.

So, let time roll on, as it does, and must, without him. As it has since the UK edition of this book was written. What you are holding is the updated U.S. version, altered, tweaked and given a shiny new postscript. It had to be done: a lot has happened since that trip to Brooklyn—and not just in the world of Trumps and Brexits and Brangelina splits. Deep Purple, rather inconsiderately, have released a new studio album.

I say 'inconsiderately' because 'Now What?!' would have been the narratively satisfying way to end the band's story.

Although its cover features a question mark and an exclamation point, it would, with its musings on old age and time, have been, more appropriately, an ideal full stop. Instead, the band completely scuppered that notion by giving us the somewhat open-ended sounding 'InFinite'. Confusingly, the accompanying tour went by the more circumscribed title of 'The Long Goodbye', so it could be that the end is near or it could be that it isn't. The album (the band's last? Maybe…who knows?) is a strong addition to Deep Purple's oeuvre and, measured purely by sales, has been their biggest hit for nearly thirty years.

One of its songs, 'Johnny's Band' resonates with the personal histories of The Good Old Boys and their like by charting the course of a pop musician's career from being 'top of the pops' to 'playing Saturday nights at The Crown'. Still, my own feeling, for what it is worth, is that, if 'InFinite' is to be Deep Purple's last recorded work, it is a less apt way to bow out than its predecessor would have been.

Speaking of bowing out—you remember that Rainbow gig that began the whole story and was supposed to have been Ritchie Blackmore's last performance on a heavy rock stage? Well, it wasn't. Blackmore being Blackmore realized that he was having way too much fun to throw in the towel just yet and decided to do it all again twelve months later.

Like the diligent and committed old rockers that we are, Tony and I bought our tickets for the tour's Birmingham stop and went along like a pair of pilgrims paying homage to a living saint. We drank our beers and ate our overpriced snack bar meals and caught up on all of each other's news before taking our seats. Sweet were the support group and were every bit as entertaining as might be expected.

When the main event finally got going, its best moment turned out to be one of the quietest: a performance—the only one on the tour—of Blackmore's tribute to Jon Lord, 'Carry On... Jon'. Coming almost exactly half a decade after the passing of the much missed maestro, it caused many a man in the audience to pretend that he'd got something in his eyes that was making them water.

For me, it was a highlight not only of that evening, but of my concert-going life.

As for the rest: it was similar fare to that served the previous year. A song or two had been dropped, others moved around, but, essentially, it was the same gig, albeit played with the added swagger that comes from repeating something that had worked well before. The packed audience didn't mind. They sang along, jumped around, waved their arms about and smiled broadly at every newly announced song. That they did more than anything else: they smiled.

Yes, Birmingham's NEC Arena was buzzing that night.

And we fans into our dotage, wherever we are around the world, will carry on buzzing too.

About The Author

ADRIAN JARVIS IS an academic and teacher. Although his interests include comics, literature, martial arts and travel, when deciding on a subject for his book, he took to heart the old adage that you should write about what you know and realised that the thing he knows most about is being a heavy rock fan. He lives in Nottingham with his wife, Karen, and his extensive collection of single malt whiskies. He spends his time trying to work out what to write about next.

CPSIA information can be obtained
at www.ICGtesting.com
Printed in the USA
FFHW021738250319
51232945-56731FF

9 781941 071816